**THE
DEAD
LADIES
PROJECT**

THE
DEAD
LADIES
PROJECT

EXILES, EXPATS,
AND EX-COUNTRIES

Jessa Crispin

The University of Chicago Press
Chicago and London

Jessa Crispin is the editor and founder of the magazines *Bookslut* and *Spolia*. She has written for the *New York Times, Guardian, Washington Post, Los Angeles Review of Books,* NPR.org, the *Chicago Sun-Times, Architect,* and other publications. She has lived in Kansas, Texas, Ireland, Chicago, Berlin, and elsewhere.

The University of Chicago Press, Chicago 60637
The University of Chicago Press, Ltd., London
© 2015 by Jessa Crispin
All rights reserved. Published 2015.
Printed in the United States of America

24 23 22 21 20 19 18 17 16 15   1 2 3 4 5
ISBN-13: 978-0-226-27845-2 (paper)
ISBN-13: 978-0-226-27859-9 (e-book)
DOI: 10.7208/chicago/9780226278599.001.0001

Library of Congress Cataloging-in-Publication Data
Crispin, Jessa, author.
    The dead ladies project : exiles, expats, and ex-countries / Jessa Crispin.
        pages cm
    Includes bibliographical references.
    ISBN 978-0-226-27845-2 (paperback : alkaline paper) —
ISBN 978-0-226-27859-9 (ebook) 1. Crispin, Jessa. 2. Cities and towns—Psychological aspects. 3. Celebrities—Homes and haunts. 4. Aliens—Biography. 5. Place (Philosophy). I. Title.
    CT120.C75 2015
    920.073—dc23
    [B]
                                                    2015013597

♾ This paper meets the requirements of ANSI/NISO Z39.48–1992 (Permanence of Paper).

for Honeybee

Contents

Prelude / Chicago

There are two Chicago cops standing in my kitchen.

They are here to take me away, and I am trying to talk them out of it. I don't know if I am doing a very good job, though, as it is hard to form a logical argument when my primary focus is on moving slowly to position myself between the cops and my oven to block their view of my stovetop. I am somehow more embarrassed about the pot of macaroni and cheese from a box, the cheap one with the sickly orange powder, than I am about their reason for being here.

The reason being that I made some threats against my life on the phone with a friend. After that I kind of bailed. It is not that I did not mean them—I was in a pretty unwashed and terrified state—it's just that saying them out loud was not part of the plan, and I felt like I could avoid the consequences of the confession simply by turning off my phone. When my friend could not get me back on the line, she called my sister, who called the police. The police came to take me to the emergency room. The emergency room doctors would then lock me away in the psych ward for observation.

And I did have a plan. The suicidal brain is good at only one thing, and that is constructing elaborate plans for doing away with itself. My plan included not telling anyone there was a problem, so that they would not interfere. Now that they had, I had to consider them in my decision. That untimely blurt is really messing things up for me.

I try to explain to the cops that I turned off my phone because it was important for me to stand weeping in front of the George Inness painting at the Art Institute, the one where the darkening world dissolves into an orange and yellow blur, not because I was swallowing drain cleaner. I mean, I made dinner—would I bother to make dinner if I were intent on ending it all? But I knew if they saw what I had made for dinner, they would cotton on to the fact that I had indeed given up on life.

Maybe I could benefit from a short hospital stay, from some time to rest and letting other people take care for a while, Jesus, yes, I am so very tired. But I see too clearly the aftermath of treatment: a hospital bill that would push me further into debt, medications I'd have to spend a year slowly trying to wean myself off. Then there is that recurring nightmare I have of being locked away, futilely trying to convince the authorities that I don't belong here, there's been some kind of mistake. I was clear on one thing: I needed a reason to live, a plan, and it had to come from within. I couldn't just let others help me find a new stability or acceptance of my circumstances. It was my circumstances that were killing me, I was sure of it.

This is how I know: no matter how securely I built my sound little structure—slowly accumulating income and a respectable writing CV, dating important men with an eye toward marriage, acquiring a varied and stimulating social life—the thought *I want to go home* would start termiting through the whole thing. How is this not my home? Is this really my life or did someone else choose it for me? Is any of this really me at all? The questions would eat at my existence until the structure collapsed into despair again and again. Every two years I would be back to this exact same spot, rebuilding my sad little sand castle in exactly the same way, surprised every time when the wave took it out. But I didn't know what else to do.

I could not explain this to the police, so instead I explained that a friend was coming over (a lie) to stay with me until I got better, I explained that I would definitely make an appointment to see a doctor (a lie), I explained that I just got overwhelmed but things were looking up. I showed calm resolve, stability and sanity, until they got the hell out of my kitchen and went away.

Perhaps the suicidal impulse was correct. But it wasn't my physical life that needed to be destroyed, only what I was doing with it.

I would need guidance, but there wasn't anyone in my life I felt I could turn to, not about this. Using my married, employed, insured friends' lives as markers for where my life should be was one of my contributing factors. That would have to go, too.

It was the dead I wanted to talk to. The writers and artists and composers who kept me company in the late hours of the night: I needed to know how they did it. I'd always been attracted to the unloosed, the wandering souls who were willing to scrape their lives clean and start again elsewhere. I needed to know how they did it, how they survived it. I couldn't do it from here, this haunted little apartment with its collection of insects and rodents, with the neighbor who sometimes goes mad and tries to break through our adjoining wall with a hammer, where the sound of gunfire comes through the window every night. No, if I was going to approach these great men and women, I would need to do it on their territory. I would have to go to them, not expect them to show up here.

Everything that was excess could be left — the Chicago apartment, the furniture, the books, the men, the social circle. There was only one thing worth keeping, and that was my work: a small literary magazine I had started a decade ago and a handful of regular writing and editing gigs. It wasn't much, but it was enough to fund train tickets and shoddy Central European sublets. And it was all portable: my whole working world existed on my laptop. It was my self that was stuck. I could unstick my-self, I thought, if I started flinging the superfluous away. The only things I really needed I could carry with me.

I would take myself to Europe and bring as my offering some spirits and the entirety of my past. Yes, I needed to talk to the dead. Maybe now that I was nearing the end, an end, maybe the dead would talk back.

Berlin / William James

Here is the real core of the religious problem: Help! Help!

WILLIAM JAMES, *Varieties of Religious Experience*

"You're in Berlin because you feel like a failure."

I had met this man all of ten minutes ago and he was already summing me up neatly. I made subtle readjustments to my clothing, as if it had been a wayward bra strap or an upwardly mobile hemline that had given me away. More likely it was my blank stare in response to his question, "So, what brings you to Berlin?"

He has had to do this a lot, I imagine: greet lost boys and girls, still wild with jet lag, still unsure how to make ourselves look less obviously like what we are, we members of the Third Great Wave of American Expatriation to Berlin. This man before me was second on the list of names that everyone gets from worried friends when resettling overseas: Everyone I Know in the City to Which You Are Moving (Not Totally Vouched For). I had lasted about a week before I sent e-mails tinged with panic to everyone on my list. He had been the first to answer.

I must have blushed at the accuracy of his remark, because he immediately qualified it. "Everyone who moves to Berlin feels like a failure. That's why we're here. You'll have good company." Still embarrassed, I scanned the menu for one of the four German words I had mastered and, failing, pointed helplessly to a random item when the waiter returned. It would prove to be a strange Swiss soda of indeterminate flavor. It tasted like the branch of a tree, carbonated. It was not unpleasant. I had been shooting for something alcoholic, but I was already too laid bare to have admitting to a mistake and reordering left in me.

At this moment it seemed unlikely this American could commiserate. My own failings were too grandiose, the depths to which I had fallen too abysmal. I was narcissistic in my failings, and he looked like he was doing pretty okay. He sat across from me confident, knowledgeable. He had ordered in German. The people in the restaurant had greeted him by name. He talked about artistic projects he was working on. He was certainly sweating less than I was on this hot July day. Later a tale would unravel, one that mimicked the stories of so many of the Americans who had flocked here over the last decade. Unable to survive financially in New York without having to abandon their writing, their art, their music, they came to a city of cheap rents, national health insurance, and plentiful bartending jobs that could cover a reasonable cost of living. He had an apartment. It had hardwood floors. A failure, my eye.

In contrast, there I was, ten days into my new city and still stumbling around like a newborn calf. I was tired of being the person I was on an almost atomic level. I longed to be disassembled, for the chemical bonds holding me together to weaken and for bits of me to dissolve slowly into the atmosphere. It was not a death wish, not really. Not anymore. I was hoping something in the environment, some sturdier, more German atoms, would replace them.

Because there does seem to be something about Berlin that calls out to the exhausted, the broke, the uninsurable with preexisting mental health disorders, the artistically spent, those trapped in the waning of careers, of inspiration, of family relations, and of ambition. To all those whose anxiety dreams play out as trying to steer a careening car while trapped in the backseat, come to us. We have a café culture and surprisingly affordable rents. Come to us, and you can finish out your collapse among people who understand.

* * *

Let's say, for a moment, that the character of a city has an effect on its inhabitants, and that it sets the frequency on which it calls out to the migratory. People who are tuned a certain way will heed the call almost without knowing why. Thinking they've chosen this city, they'll never know that the city chose them. Let's say, for a moment, that the literal situation of a city can leak out into the metaphorical realm. That the city is the vessel and we are all merely beings of differing viscosity, slowly taking on the shape of that into which we are poured.

If that were the case, what to make of the fact that Berlin is built on sand? Situated on a plain with no natural defenses, no major river, no wealth of any particular resource, it's a city that should not exist. It can't be any wonder that Berlin has for hundreds of years—no, longer than that, past Napoleon, past the medieval days when suspected witches were lined up at the city gates and molten metal was poured between their clenched teeth, past the whispers of the Romans that those who inhabited these lands were not quite human, back to the days of the people residing here who are now known to us only by some pottery shards and bronze tools—been a little unstable. It would explain the city's endless need to collapse and rebuild, even as the nation that engulfs it marches on confidently, linearly.

Perhaps its unstable nature is what beckons the unstable to its gates. The Lausitzer. The Jastorf. The Semnonen. The nameless and the preliterate. A shifting bunch of conquerors and the conquered. On through invaders and defenders, and populations reduced by half in war, disease, and the destruction of whoever pulled the short straw for being the scapegoat this century. The process merely sped up in the twentieth, oscillating madly through world wars and grotesque ideas, crashing economies and blind eyes turned.

It plays out seasonally as well here in the northern reaches of Germany. The lush highs of summer, everything green and tangled with a sun reluctant to leave its post at night and overly enthusiastically trying to rouse you from bed in the very early hours of the morning, crash endlessly down toward the darkness of the winter solstice. The trees that had been blooming in a state of fecund glory when I arrived in the city lost their leaves, revealing that the only things behind them were the endless concrete boxes of Soviet midcentury "architecture." The sun shunned us and rarely peeked out from behind its thick cloud cover. When it deigned to, it gave off all the glow and heat of a porch light. The gray of the sky matched the gray of the buildings matched the gray of the thick coating of ice that remained on the sidewalks all winter. I fell on it one night, or early one morning, I guess, a little worse for wear, accompanied by a man I met at a bar, whose entire seduction strategy was just to follow me home, despite the fact that I kept trying to shoo him away like a stray dog.

I was six months into my Berlin residence. And from my akimbo position I threw the holy tantrum of a sailor-mouthed two-year-old. "Fuck this city. Fuck it. Why the fuck did I ever move here, god fucking damn it."

"You're strange," said the German man, still resolutely standing by.

"Help me up."

That's when I took my William James essays off the shelf. I found in his works of philosophy a friend, a mentor, a professor, and some sort of idealized father. It was his works on the more mundane matters that I relied on—how to make changes in your life, how to believe you can make changes in your life, how to convince yourself to get out of bed in the morning, how not to be a worthless slug—rather than his more important pieces about war or whatever.

James is now a bit of an odd fellow in philosophy. More widely influential than widely known, his theory of pragmatism and his groundbreaking work in the field of psychology make him something of a hidden mover. If you do seek him out, it's not generally in the way one reads Descartes or Kant or Nietzsche, as a refinement of the intellect or in the pursuit of one's studies. One finds James when one needs him. He makes quiet sense of the world in all its glories and deprivations, its calamities and its beauties. As a philosopher, James is able to hold all of the sorrow and violence and pain of the world in his mind and remain somehow optimistic. It doesn't wipe out the goodness of the world, it just sits beside it. It's no wonder then that people get a little religious about this agnostic philosopher, this man who can restore your faith in the world without necessarily bringing god into it.

I sought out William James because I needed him. He and I were now separated by about a century of death, but we found ourselves occupying the same biographical eddy: bottoming out in Berlin.

* * *

Here is how William James found himself in Berlin: a failure. He had tried and failed to become a painter, failed to become a doctor, failed to become an adventurer. He was not yet a writer, but he was almost certainly still a virgin. He was in his mid-twenties and painfully aware that he had failed even in deciding what it was he wanted to do. He stood there, absolutely calcified with indecision and doubt, while his soon-to-be-famous friends like Oliver Wendell Holmes Jr. made decisions and started careers, and his soon-to-be-famous younger brother, Henry, started his literary apprenticeship with *the Atlantic*.

Whereas he—well, he fled. First to Dresden and then to Berlin. He arrived under the pretext of furthering his education, but that may have simply been a way to convince his parents to pay for the trip because, despite his advancing age, he had yet to make an income. At any rate, he failed to go to class, ever. Instead he holed up in his Berlin guesthouse, learning German, training his telescope on the legs of the occupants of the all-girls' school across the street, and failing to figure out a way to flirt with the pretty woman who played the piano downstairs. All the while in his letters to his brother he was alluding to a daily battle not to do himself in.

James lightly fictionalized this time in his life in *Varieties of Religious Experience*, passing off the breakdown to someone he knows who told him about it. (He's French, you don't know him.) In that work he described the sensation of his suicidal idyll as "desperation absolute and complete, the whole universe coagulating about the sufferer into a material of overwhelming horror, surrounding him without opening or end. Not the conception or intellectual perception of evil, but the grisly blood-freezing heart-palsying sensation of it close upon one, and no other conception or sensation able to live for a moment in its presence." And while his letters to his parents hint at some of this darkness, there he mostly chats about that other Berlin experience, the roast veal and the beer and the music and the philosophy.

Here is how Berlin responded to William James's time in Berlin: they built a center in his name. At the place of his greatest misery and torment, they built a permanent structure. Although maybe at this point they couldn't help it. After all the documentation they had to do of the horrors of the twentieth century, maybe now it's an unconscious reflex to throw up a memorial on the site of every trauma.

Well, not really a structure, I guess. More like a small room. The minute I learned of the center's existence, I sent off an e-mail to make an appointment. I expected a hall of philosophy on the university campus, maybe in that glorious red brick so many of the buildings in James's time had been constructed with. I scribbled the address down on a piece of paper, and I took the train to the outskirts, to the University of Potsdam campus. It's situated next to Sanssouci and its gardens, the former playground of the Prussian king. While the main path through the gardens is still marked with magnificent elm trees, most of the grounds have been allowed to go to seed. It's not a tourist destination on par with Versailles, and so it is kept in only middling shape. There is a lovely rose garden, but that is surrounded by tangle and bramble. It's been let go in the Berlin way, all of those straight German lines blurring a little into chaos.

Past the garden gates, into the campus, into the main philosophy hall, up the main staircase, down a hallway, to the left and then right, I came to my destination. It was a small door. The William James Center proved, despite its authoritative name, to be the work of one man. Herr Doktor Professor Logi Gunnarsson. Or is it Herr Professor Doktor . . . I should have remembered to look up the proper order before I left. "It's Logi, call me Logi." Luckily Dr. Logi is Icelandic and not beholden to the German titling system. The center's archives are really just the contents of Dr. Logi's office. A desk, a computer, some bookcases. Dr. Logi is slight and sandy, and he has the wonderful awkwardness that comes with too many hours spent in the company of dead men.

He is, he tells me, attempting to re-create William James's personal library as part of his administration of the center, so that he can be surrounded by the same books that surrounded James. It's a devotional act couched in a scholarly one. It's an act I can understand. Dr. Logi pours me a cup of tea, and we chat about our good friend William James. Up for discussion, a traumatic encounter with a prostitute, alluded to in letters to his brother and in a journal. He did, it seems, either lose his virginity to the prostitute or, perhaps even more traumatically, fail to.

"The poor dear," I say.

"Yes, quite. He was hopeless with women. It seems, though, that after he married Alice Howe Gibbens, the physical ailments he was treating in Berlin, the bad back and so on, disappeared."

"Were they caused by the burden of a protracted virginity?"

"Perhaps. The poor dear."

I am keeping Dr. Logi from professional duties, but I don't care and it appears he doesn't either. I imagine it might be a relief for him, as it is for me, to have someone to converse with about our favorite person. Or willingly converse, as I'm sure he inflicts William James on the people around him like I do.

"What do you make," I ask slowly, "of the fact that his first book wasn't published until he was forty-nine?"

Part of William's freakout, Dr. Logi had mentioned earlier, sprang from an enormous need to be *seen*. By the public, by his friends, by his father. He wanted to "assert his reality" on the world, as he wrote in his letters, and it took approximately twenty years after writing that statement until he would.

"Surely not . . ." Dr. Logi starts, but then he does the math in his head. "I guess I knew that but had forgotten. I mean . . . And he could not have known he would eventually succeed."

We both sit quietly, drinking the dregs of our tea and feeling the long expanse of the years before us. The weight of uncertainty. Whether it'll be a late blooming or whether the soil will prove to be infertile.

* * *

Whenever James was corresponding with a colleague or an inquirer, Dr. Logi told me, he would request from them a portrait. It was important for him to see the whole of the person, at least a bit of their humanity, and not only their written representation.

In that spirit, I have before me two images of William James. The first was taken around the time he moved to Berlin. He looks stricken, pale and withdrawn. It is as if he had recoiled into a permanent flinch. He looks off to the side, unable perhaps to meet the camera's gaze. There is something fractured deep at the heart of him.

In the other, it is a few decades on. There is gray in his beard and his face is worn. He exudes charm, warmth, and wisdom. It is a William James in whose lap you want to sit and listen to stories. He is keeping some secrets, but he will share them if you draw near.

It is the distance between these two photographs that is so fascinating. Not simply in age but in substance of the man. Biographers are interested (I am interested) in the Berlin breakdown because of the distance traveled between the two Jameses and the quality of the end result. It's a favorite myth in our culture that hardship makes you a better person, that it is merely the grindstone on which your essence is refined and polished. But the truth is that scarcity, depression, thwarted ambition, and suffering most often leave the person a little twisted. That is the territory where mean drunks and tyrannical bastards come from.

Not so with James. He may have always been a little hopeless with women (he sent a series of hilarious and heartbreaking letters to his Alice in the months before their wedding, in a vein that will be instantly recognizable to anyone who has ever gotten a little sullen after a bottle of wine and decided to start texting), and the weight of depression did occasionally re-descend, but he walked out of that phase with dignity and great compassion. He used his experiences, both the good and the ill, for the base of his incredibly humane body of work.

So then what's the magic formula? Can his transition be distilled down to a scientific protocol to be reproduced at home in your own basement laboratory? Could we use William James's example to turn our respective chemical imbalances into alchemical processes?

* * *

There are persons whose existence is little more than a series of zig-zags, as now one tendency and now another gets the upper hand. Their spirit wars with their flesh, they wish for incompatibles. Wayward impulses interrupt their most deliberate plans, and their lives are one long drama of repentance and an effort to repair misdemeanors and mistakes.

WILLIAM JAMES, *Varieties of Religious Experience*

It is difficult today to imagine the Berlin that James encountered in the nineteenth century. So much of the city was reduced to rubble and ash in the intervening years. I can look at photos and get a sense of who the city might have been. But when I'm out, actually walking around on the streets, it is an entirely different place.

Most of the surface of the city was bulldozed after World

War II, and the unsalvageable and the unclaimed was dumped in Grunewald on the outskirts of town. The pile of junk that used to be houses, used to be bakeries and hat shops, used to be attached to human bodies, was covered in dirt, and the wild was allowed to reclaim it. Now it is something of a park or nature preserve, with hiking trails through the woods—the trees still looking suspiciously young—up and down this artificial hill. One of the only hills in this swamp-turned-into-a-city.

The Germans may look like proper churchgoing Lutherans on the outside, but they are all at heart tree-worshiping animists from way back, starting with the pagan cults in the Schwarzwald, to the nature idolatry of the romantic and counter-Enlightenment movements in the nineteenth century. It still bleeds through in their songs and in their art. A few decades before James arrived, Bogumil Goltz wrote, "What the evil over-clever, insipid, bright cold world encumbers and complicates, the wood-green mysterious, enchanted, dark, culture-renouncing but true to the law of nature must free and make good again."

So maybe that is where James's Berlin still resides, out in Grunewald, buried in some sort of purification rite inspired by a mysterious calling from deep within the German DNA. The wood-green making all of those horrors good again. It's a calm place, soothing. But also policed by territorial wild boar.

* * *

Stefan is giving me important life advice over cocktails. I should be taking notes. Stefan is building an opera house, or, I guess, overseeing the building of an opera house, and that seems like the type of person you should take seriously. He has in front of him a small glass of one of these Deutsche herbal liqueurs. It is the color of garnets and it tastes like a potion. I am drinking a French 75, which I will retroactively feel shameful about later, after I learn the cocktail was not actually, as I believed, named after a really good year but takes its name from a French cannon used against the Germans in World War I. I wonder if this is why, in this Berlin bar, it is served strangely tinted red.

The bar is from the 1920s, all dark wood and red wallpaper, heavy drapery and cigarette smoke. The mystery of the place is heightened if you take the shortcut through the courtyard of some residential buildings. It looks like a dead end on Google Maps, but you can weave your way through. You could go the long way and stay on well-lit commercial streets, but then it no longer feels like a secret. Outside the bar is a poster for a performance of *Cabaret*—a German version of an American man's musical version of a British man's version of Weimar Berlin. Bob Fosse remains the link between my previous home of Chicago and my new.

I have trouble listening when Stefan is speaking, and not only because the bar tonight is loud and overcrowded, which it is. There is an army of white boys at the bar, drinking beer and wearing an almost identical uniform of trainers, jeans, and dark gray hoodie. My real problem is that Stefan's hair is so beautiful, so silvered and swooshing and glorious, that I have to sit on my hands to keep from forcing them into his mane. Shit, what's that he's saying?

"Don't end up like Bertolt Brecht."

That seems like horrible advice. Shouldn't the goal of life be to end up as close to Bertolt Brecht as possible? I need a little context.

"When Brecht moved to Los Angeles, he had such a difficult time learning English that he gave up. It soured him, being unable to communicate, and he started to hate America. Read his journals, you'll see."

For Stefan, every topic of conversation circles back to Bertolt Brecht, the way for me every topic of conversation circles back to William James. I take his point, which is made in impeccable English, shaming me further. I have been stubborn about learning to speak German. It feeds into my unsettled state. Why learn German if I'm only going to be here for a few years? But then how can I know if I want to stay unless I assimilate a little and give the place a chance? It is mortifying when someone addresses me in German I can't follow, and yet part of me likes the little bubble I live in, the way I can tune out conversations on the subway because I can't follow them anyway.

"Read Brecht's journals," Stefan repeats. "And learn German."

* * *

I do read Brecht's journals—translated into English. When he does write about America, it's occasionally to complain about the FBI coming around to talk to him, and I wonder if that had as much of an impact on his displeasure with the country as his difficulty learning the language.

On March 23, 1942, he wrote:

remarkable how in this place a universally depraving, cheap prettiness prevents people from living in a halfway cultivated fashion, ie living with dignity. in my garden-house in utting, and even under my danish thatched roof, it was possible to browse over the bellum gallicum in the morning, here it would be utter snobbery. lidingö saw the discussions of the 20 on the mistakes made in spain, a few discussions with ljungdal on hegel's dialectics, the young workers' little masked theatre which performed HOW MUCH IS YOUR IRON? finland had marlebäk with the birch coppice round the house, the coffee hour in the main farmhouse after a sauna, and the two-room flat in the harbour quarter of helsinki, packed with good people. there was room for diderot and the epigrams of meleagros as well as marx. here you feel like francis of assisi in an aquarium, lenin in the prater (or at the munich oktoberfest), a chrysanthemum in a coalmine or a sausage in a greenhouse. the country is quite big enough to squeeze all other countries out of one's memory. one could write dramas if it didn't itself have any or need any, but it has all that, if in the most negligible condition. mercantilism produces everything, but in the form of saleable goods, so here art is ashamed of its usefulness, but not of its exchange value.

It reminds me of the inevitable line of complaint you hear whenever a group of American expats gather in Berlin. About the invasive nosiness of the Germans, about the way the pinched old lady who lives upstairs is always watching you and probably taking notes, about the way Germans stare at you on the street, on the subway, even in the saunas which will be of course both naked and coed, the way they don't respect your personal space, the way grocery stores are closed on Sundays because the government at some point decided they'd rather women be at home with their families that day and now you can't buy milk when you need it, the way they scold you publicly if you cross the street against the light, the way if you go to the pharmacy to buy antacids you are more likely to leave having heard a lecture about the importance of a healthy diet than with the actual tablets. These complaints occasionally tip over into the word *Stasi*, the word *Nazi*. No one is proud of these moments.

But no one is immune to this impulse to romanticize where you came from—where people did things that made sense, goddammit—when faced with a new culture from which you are out of step. It's easy to respond to the foreignness of your new home with indignation and "Why, I never!" James's letters home grow more and more flummoxed as he tries to learn German and interact with the natives. "The language is infernal," he complains to his family.

"German requires . . . that you should bring all the resources of your nature, of every kind, to a focus, and hurl them again and again on the sentence, till at last you feel something give way, as it were, and the Idea begins to unravel itself."

William must have had to bring all the resources of his nature to hurl against the German personality as well, if his experience at all resembled mine. So many hours I've spent dissecting evenings out with German men, just to determine whether or not it had been a date. "Well, he paid, but he did not touch me, and that's the fifth paying-but-no-touching dinner and for Christ's sake I have met his family what the fuck is going on!"

A friend once intervened. "If a German man likes you, he won't touch you, because he respects you. If he just wants to be friends, he won't touch you. Basically during the first ten dates he'll only touch you if he doesn't care much for you." And meanwhile they will sit there wrapped in their beautiful impenetrability, never flashing enough vulnerability to let you know if your own advance will be met with anything other than stony silence. It is baffling. Someone should develop a code of hand signals.

I wonder if James tried to make a move on a Teutonic woman during his residency, and if he was frozen by that aloofness. Though, in his letters, he seems just as desperate for the company of men as for the affections of women. He wrote home, "Berlin is a bleak and unfriendly place. The inhabitants are rude and graceless, but must conceal a solid worth beneath it. I only know seven of them, and they are the elite. It is very hard getting acquainted with them, as you have to make all the advances yourself, and your antagonist shifts so between friendliness and a drill sergeant in formal politeness that you never know exactly on what footing you stand with them."

There was always something that worked sadly in William, to borrow his expression: a loneliness that put him on unequal footing with men he tried to befriend. There is an element of grasping panic in his letters to Oliver Wendell Holmes Jr., as William begs for swifter response. He was in his own bubble in Berlin, unable to communicate, unable to force communication from back home, alone with his thoughts, none of which were good. He could have been standing in the center of Unter den Linden, arms outstretched, his entire psyche unzipped and his tremendous need spilling out of him, and the Germans would have simply brushed past him, without even the slightest *Schuldigen* in passing.

*　*　*

I'm not allowed to leave the university campus with the volumes of James's letters, so I read them outside, under a tree. Surrounded by twenty-year-olds, all of them seeming happily grouped up, greeting friends with a double cheek kiss and enthusiastic smiles. When my back starts to ache, a reminder of the age difference between them and me, I return the books to Dr. Logi's office, I take the train back to Alexanderplatz, and then I walk the mile home. To an empty apartment, furnished with someone else's belongings.

I make a cup of tea, I check my e-mail, and I feel the poreless surface of the bubble around me. I want to bend time and snatch William out of his lonely guesthouse. I could use the company. But I know how his story ends. He has to stay in Berlin a bit longer so that he can become a great man. And me? Who knows what the fuck I'm doing.

Every James biographer has a slightly different take on the breakdown, but there is near universal agreement that it has something to do with his father, Henry James Sr.

I have to say that I do not like his father. In fact, I dislike him with such intensity that it's clear I am projecting some of my own issues there. He always struck me as being the worst kind of philosopher, even besides the fact that he never had an original thought in his life. He held everyone to ridiculously high standards—his two eldest sons especially—while never once noticing how far from his own mark he fell. His own philosophical framework was either an exercise in great hypocrisy—praising work as the path of true manhood and self-sufficiency while he himself lived off his father's fortune and never held a job—or an act of self-justification: warping theological thought so that the waywardness of sinning, such as his own drinking problem and lusts, was actually somehow a path to becoming more divine. He preached that parents must allow their children to be their own selves and make their own way, and yet he demanded total obedience and deference from his children. In short, he constructed his philosophy as a way to avoid ever experiencing a moment of self-doubt or questioning.

As the eldest son, William felt enormous pressure both to please his father and to achieve a level of respectability and renown. There was a burden on him not to disappoint and not to fail. The problem was that his father's definition of failure kept expanding to encompass anything William tried to do. Henry Sr. was supportive when his sons dabbled in interests, but when they decided on a specific course of action, their chosen field was suddenly never good enough, never important enough, never worthy of his sons' great potential. His father discouraged William at every turn, and so he skipped from profession to profession, trying to make contact with his father's approval, only to have it yanked away like Lucy's football, again and again.

Henry Jr. noticed this perverse tendency in their father, reflecting that the message they received was never to dismiss "any suggestion of an alternative." He continues in his memoirs, "What we were to do instead was just *be* something, something unconnected with specific doing, something free and uncommitted, something finer in short than being *that*, whatever it was, might consist of." Henry Sr. wanted his sons to live in a space of limitless potentiality, while he continued to judge them harshly on the lack of concrete results.

"Every person gets the father they require" to turn into the people they need to be, a colleague once said to me, but this colleague has flowy hair, wears a lot of purple, and uses words like *fate* and *destiny* in an enviably sincere and unironic way. But here's the truth: it was these decades of indecision that made William James unique. Later he was able to draw on his art training, his medical training, his philosophical learning, his spiritual experimentation, his psychology background to create a philosophy rooted in body, soul, and mind. And without a crazymaking father forcing him in one direction and then another, he never would have, goddammit, lived up to his full potential. That doesn't mean I do not still sometimes yell at William James's father in my head when I am reading their letters.

A friend just back from Latvia told me that the way the Russians dealt with the mosquitoes there, big as hummingbirds, was to lace their own food and the food of their livestock with insecticides. They would poison themselves and their own property to kill off the parasites. With a parent like Henry Sr. it would be possible to take the Russians' lead, to poison your own ambition so that no one undeserving could lay claim to your success. But then I was always more spiteful than James was; I doubt the thought occurred to him.

* * *

I am conscious of a desire I never had before so strongly or so permanently, of narrowing and deepening the channel of my intellectual activity, of economizing my feeble energies and consequently treating with more respect the few things I shall devote them to. This temper may be a transient one . . . but

something tells me that practically my salvation depends . . . on
following such a plan.

WILLIAM JAMES, journal, Berlin

I moved to Berlin with my life distilled down to two suitcases.
I'm still not sure if that was an act of pessimism or optimism.
The rest was hauled away by my new Craigslist friends, while I
drank vodka on ice and nodded when they asked, "Are you sure
this is free?" Nothing went into storage, nothing was given to
friends to hold onto just in case this scheme didn't work out and
I needed to come back. Maybe in the end it'll be one of those
defining moments that makes all the difference in retrospect.
Who knows how long it'll take for me to get far enough away
to tell. But I can't help that when I come across the Fool card
in the tarot, with his funny hat and little dog, boldly stepping
off the edge of the cliff, trusting the universe will catch him, I
always picture his body dashed to pieces on the rocks below.

After all, throwing away all my belongings wasn't really part
of the plan. It's just that when I started to pack, I looked around
and found only two suitcases' worth of things that merited
saving.

Pessimism, James would write in a later essay, a few years
after he wrote the world's first psychology textbook, *The Prin-
ciples of Psychology* (that first book that changed everything,
both in the world and in his life), is a spiritual problem. It is a
crying out to the heavens to be proved wrong, or at least struck
down already. After all, a realist would know that there's a
whole array of possibilities that could result from every small
decision. Being impaled on a tree branch at the bottom of a
ravine is, yes, one potential outcome, but it's not going to happen every time. That deep cynicism springs from a "religious
demand to which there comes no religious reply."

There is very little of the abstract in James's writing, interested as he was in the full-bodied living of life. His comment about pessimism was included in an essay titled "Is Life Worth Living?" written nearly three decades after his time in Germany.

"He wrote that essay when he was suicidally depressed, you know." I was in a large hotel bed with a man. Pre-Berlin. Part of the content of my life I did not want to take with me across the Atlantic. Who knows where my blue dress had landed, although I guess it does not matter. This was my hotel room, not his. The heavy breathing had barely slowed before he began talking about William James again, continuing the conversation that had begun in the hotel bar. I was starting to wonder how I was going to get him to leave. "Or, I guess, he was coming out of being suicidally depressed, and there he was addressing this lecture to a room of young students. He wrote that essay because he was trying to find the answer."

I think of James as he might have been on that April day. Jacket off. Shirtsleeves rolled up. Sweat on his pale brow. Clutching the lectern to hide the shaking of his hands. Cracking jokes ("it depends on the liver") while very seriously deciding whether to do away with himself. Maybe he thought back to the pit into which he had fallen in Berlin, when "thoughts of the pistol, the dagger, and the bowl began to usurp an unduly large part" of his attention. I wonder if everything that had happened in the intervening years—the fame that came with his first book, the lovely wife, the prestigious position at Harvard— seemed ultimately hollow. If even all of that could not keep him buoyed, what could its true value be? Maybe he thought he should have just gotten it over with all those years ago.

Or maybe he was actually doing okay and this guy didn't know what he was talking about. Maybe I should not consider post-sex conversation with men I don't care for "historical research."

What is it with me and men and William James? I only started reading him because I had a crush on a boy. A boy who wore a hemp necklace. My romantic degradation knows no bounds. He had announced at dinner one night, out of the blue, that *Varieties of Religious Experience* was his favorite non-fiction book of all time. It was not the first mention of James; for months his name had been cropping up all around me. I would see him quoted in books I was reading, friends would reference him in conversation. But I had always figured yuck, an East Coast dead white philosopher? who taught at Harvard? Not for me. It took a pretty face (and a hemp necklace) before I broke down and read *Varieties*. And then everything changed.

Maybe the universe is just as exasperated as I am that it has to put its messages in mouths I want to put on mine before I notice its extraordinary efforts at synchronicity.

* * *

My home in Berlin is built on sand, so it's not like I've spent a lot of money gussying up the place.

"The opera house is sinking into the ground," Stefan tells me. "Of course it is."

My belongings still amount to only a little more than two suitcases. I carry my passport on me at all times, like some sort of international fugitive trying to evade Interpol. My relationship with this city is renegotiated on a daily basis. It is a strange way to live.

The freeing sensation that comes with burning your old life down to the foundations fades surprisingly quickly. At the first sign of rain, you will miss that old roof, inadequate as it might have been. And so there were nights, as I lay sleepless in a bed I did not own, staring at a painting I did not choose, when I requested the presence of William James. And he would come, the older, more confident version, the one who could see his life in retrospect, in a three-piece suit and smoking a pipe. (I don't know where the pipe came from—it's possible I'm confusing him with my father.) Sometimes he would just sit on the edge of my bed and squeeze my foot through the blanket until I got back to sleep. At other times we would talk. Mostly about the loneliness that is so deep it leads you into conversation with people who are dead.

At those times he would rest his kind eyes on me. "Consider this to be the gloaming," he would say. "When it's too dark to navigate by the landscape. And it will get darker still, but then you'll be able to navigate by the heavens."

In the midst of his own time in the gloaming, James stumbled upon the revelation that he had free will to direct his own life. It was a philosophical concept, but I doubt it was coincidence that this idea struck him as he first began to challenge his father and reject the beliefs bestowed upon him. "My first act of free will shall be to believe in free will," he wrote in his journal on that day. It must have been the first sighting of the North Star. He still spent the next few years in the dark, falling over things and getting depressed. But he was oriented. He was moving in a single direction that would bring him to a good end.

* * *

Once you've been in Berlin for more than three months—a successful trip to the Ausländerbehörde is usually the starting point—you will start showing up in people's lists, Everyone I Know in the City to Which You Are Moving. The longer you stay, the more lists you will appear on, and the looser the ties will be between you and the new resident. You will buy coffee, you will soothe panic. You will pick up on certain patterns and gain an ability to guess how long someone will stay based on their answers to a few basic questions.

"Did you leave your things in storage in the States?" If yes, they'll be gone in six months. If you have a safety net, you're probably going to use it after that first visa meeting, that first month of winter, that first ten-page mandatory health insurance application printed in very small German.

"Do you know someone who lives here?" If they came because they have friends in the city, they'll leave around the same time their friends do, which they will, because it's Berlin and almost everyone leaves.

"So. What brings you to Berlin?" If the question brings out that hollow stare, the blank expression, you know they're going to be here for a while, at least as long as it takes to sort a few things out.

When James left Berlin, he returned to the States to finish his medical degree and then join the Harvard faculty. Now there's a building on campus named after him. I'm still looking for my home, and it's time to head off again. After a few glasses of wine I start looking up apartment listings in Trieste, in Galway, in St. Petersburg. I wonder which one of them I might call home in the same way I call Berlin home, that is, the "for now" remains silent. I wonder what it's like over there, and what I would be like over there.

Trieste / Nora Barnacle

Wives became strangers
to me, enemies.

EDNA O'BRIEN

On an October evening in 1904, Nora Barnacle and James Joyce stepped off the train in Trieste at the end of a long journey that had begun on the docks of a Dublin harbor.

Nora took their bags and stationed herself in the little park across from the Bahnhof's entrance, while James went to make their arrangements. They had arrived with only the barest of logistics figured out: a promise of a teaching position that would turn out to be pure fantasy, a vague idea of the city's layout. But for now James, confident in their future in Trieste, went off to secure a place to stay for himself and the woman who would become his wife.

Nora settled in to wait. And wait. The sun set, and still no James. The usual drunks and layabouts wandered through the darkened square, and still no James. Late night turned into early morning, and still no James. He had taken all of their money, so for now her options were limited to the confines of the city square. She waited for her lover to return.

Let's leave Nora there for the moment. Chilled, or maybe not. Panicked, or maybe not. Let's leave James wherever he may be, and his biographers all have different theories about where he was waylaid. Was he cavorting with prostitutes? Was he off drinking with sailors? Had he been arrested and was being held in police custody?

Whatever the specifics were that night—and if I really wanted to I am sure I could find all sorts of facts to flesh out the anecdote, what the temperature was as Nora waited outside through the night, what time the sun set, what time the sun rose, from which direction the wind was blowing—no amount of digging through the written record will help us get into the experience of Nora Barnacle, waiting for the man she just crossed half of Europe for, unmarried and therefore unprotected legally, as this flake got distracted by one shiny bauble or another. We can't spill out the contents of her head or take the measure of her emotional state.

But my reluctance to tell the story straight has more to do with me than it has to do with Nora. That is how it generally goes with these artists' wives.

* * *

Consider the position of the wife. Unless the genius under consideration married late in his career and ended up with a fan or a secretary for a wife, as many creative male geniuses do, the genius marries a woman *as a man*. Not as the divine being that we, the audience, worship and make our sacrifices to. The genius marries as a physical body who spills his tea, who gets a bit sloppy when he hits the gin, who when choosing between spending their last dollar on food or on paint will oftentimes choose paint. The audience is left out of that part of it. We see the output, not the intake. And being greedy little fuckers, we see anything that does not facilitate that output as an obstacle.

So we have mixed feelings about the wife. When she is muse, when she takes dictation, when she is the facilitator and the midwife, we love her. When she is the nag, when she insists that her husband find paying work so he doesn't drag her and their children through another hungry and cold winter, when she throws him out of the house for being a drunk bully, we hate her. But all we see from the cheap seats is what we collectively decide to see. If our favorite artist was a rapist, a drunk, a Nazi, a wife-beater, a murderer—and so many of them were—we do a complicated emotional calculus to find a reason to keep their paintings on our museum walls and their books on our shelves. We can justify almost anything as long as we still get access to that life-changing work. Leo Tolstoy raped his wife? William S. Burroughs shot his in the head? Roman Polanski (allegedly!) anally raped a thirteen-year-old girl? What does it mean in the grand scheme of things, I mean really?

But the wife. If she becomes a hindrance, if she throws a canvas into the fire in a fit of rage or interrupts the genius as a new poem is forming in his subconscious, thus losing it forever, that we cannot forgive. That must be why I have seen Nora referred to as an illiterate, a bore, a whore. Nora's great crime was that she did not fall in love with James Joyce the genius. She fell in love with James Joyce the man.

* * *

"Nora Barnacle is not a very interesting person." So said Richard Ellmann, author of the definitive James Joyce biography, to Brenda Maddox, author of the only Nora Barnacle biography, who quoted him to me.

In a way Ellmann is correct. Nora Barnacle grew up in Galway, Ireland, in a working-class Irish family. She worked as a chambermaid in a convent and then moved to Dublin, where she met James. She followed him to Trieste, then to Zurich, then to Paris, then back to Zurich. We are interested in her only because of James, because he turned her into Molly Bloom in *Ulysses* and Anna Livia in *Finnegans Wake*. Had they never met, Nora would have simply faded away like any other mortal woman, remembered in old family photo albums and as a name on a genealogy report. But they did meet. And James did transform her stories and her conversation, her bawdy jokes and memories of a western Irish childhood into some of the greatest novels of the twentieth century. And so James is the filter through which we see Nora, and James is the filter through which Nora gained access to the world.

But Nora Barnacle is the only reason I am interested in Trieste, a little city nestled in the farthest crook of the Adriatic. A little city now known only for its famous husbands, the great men who lived and died here: James Joyce, Italo Svevo, Richard Francis Burton, Stendahl. Trieste spastically reminds everyone who will pay attention of its former consorts, naming every square, every thoroughfare, every street, every staircase after one of them.

Trieste is not very interesting, but it's not interesting in the way spaghetti with clams is not very interesting. It is comforting, it is simple, it jacks up my internal serotonin supply, and it would insulate my body with ten extra pounds of butterfat if I were not staying at the very top of a six-floor walk-up at the very top of a very steep hill.

* * *

"There is no such place in our system." But first I had to get to Trieste, which was something of a problem. Deutsche Bahn did not recognize it as an actual place, or they were doing that thing where if I did not phrase my question in exactly the right order with exactly the right words they were going to pretend like they had no idea what I was talking about. Communicating with Germans is like playing one long text adventure game, only the goal was never a princess in a castle, it's something mundane like getting your electric bill paid so you can continue to have lights in your apartment.

"Well, it's near Venice." *It used to be Austrian!* I want to say, but I'm not totally up to date on Austro-German tensions, and I don't want to make the situation with the DB employee in the very sharp red vest any worse.

"I can get you to Venice. At Venice you can buy a ticket to Trieste."

"Is that a thing? Or are you guessing?"

"You can probably buy a train ticket to Trieste in Venice."

I figured being adrift in Venice would never make the list of the great tragedies that can befall a human being, and so I booked the overnight trip over the Alps. I hoped Trieste still existed. Everyone seemed to agree that Trieste had had its heyday and that it was awhile back now. Pre–World War I, even. After the Austro-Hungarian Empire ceased to exist, Trieste kind of blipped out of everyone's consciousness. But maybe all that psychic chatter—thoughts, conversation, prayer, written words—about a city helps it keep its physical form. Maybe with too much neglect and thoughtlessness the place begins to dissolve into the sea and lose its place in the earthly realm. Maybe it can cause a city to go ghost overnight.

But there it was, after a mostly sleepless night, sweating silently in my private train cabin in the late June heat. I saw it coming around the bend from Venice, the train almost entirely empty by now. The sea was upon us, a glittering, blinding thing. We passed Trieste's cursed Habsburg castle and slid into the station. As I hauled my bag to the taxi line, I looked up to see a little park across from the station entrance. There was no tall redhead still sitting on her trunk, but then this was the wrong station. The nineteenth-century station was farther south. There were only a few daytime drunks and white boys with dreads kicking a ball around, waiting for whatever bus to take them wherever next.

I had someplace specific to go. I had one address at which

to pick up the keys and another at which I would be staying. It was a near-empty little studio with two plastic plates, two chipped glasses, three forks—in case I wanted to throw a party, I guess—and no corkscrew. But it was mine for one month. I found it, I paid for it. I could take my luggage directly there. I let the taxi driver lift my bag into the trunk and we drove off, without even a glance back toward that park.

* * *

Of all the places James took Nora, Trieste was her favorite. Trieste was in its finest bloom then. Here Nora was not the wife of the genius, she was the partner of the man, and she became the mother of two children. James may have already been a genius—here he finished *Portrait of the Artist* and began work on *Ulysses*—but for now the outside world was not taking note. Here they were surrounded by family, not acolytes. Here she was Nora, not Molly or Anna, nor the wife people pretended to care about in order to get access to the husband. Here in Trieste, in the quiet, she had her domain. She had a home.

* * *

In every new city I need one routine, one repetition, and that's how the city unlocks itself for me. One café visited two days in a row with identical orders. One route through the city blazed and followed. One morning ritual with variations from my home ritual established. My Trieste routine was cocktail hour. At 5 p.m. I set aside the work on my magazine to walk the thirty minutes north to the city center. And yet to get from one neighborhood to another is to walk through countless centuries and through the domains of countless Triestine conquerors.

The Italian Trieste I live in, a neighborhood built up after the war, is all grandmothers leaning out of their third-floor windows dangling massive, carb-loaded bosoms and hoses attached to kitchen faucets to water their ground-level sidewalk-adjacent gardens from on high. It is Vespas and hair gel and clouds of tacky cologne that smells of the rutting of domesticated animals and gets trapped in the dense humid air, clinging to you like a mist. It is gelato shops and sidewalk cafés, everyone scooting their chair as the day passes to remain in the shifting blocks of shade.

As you pass through a wooded park, suddenly the Illyrians from who knows how far back are present and accounted for, ancient and primal, as the sun purifies every surface and distills it down to its essential aroma. You can smell the trees, the dirt; even the baking rocks give off a fragrance. Walking through the small park brings out tree-dwelling ancestral DNA reflexes, the intensity of the earthiness filling your lungs and calling you out for the primate you are. Every time the wind shifts you get hit with a different smell, and it digs into your hippocampus, excavating passing moments, a long-dead love flying just through your periphery until the wind shifts again and you're in your childhood kitchen, sticking your fingers into something once alive and now roasted, and then you are somewhere else, in another time.

As you approach the heart of the city, the first irritation of civilization that these other layers soothed themselves around, it is ancient Rome's Tergeste. All crumbled edges and collapsing columns. A medieval church stands there with gilded mosaics and the bones of saints, an altar to the Virgin Mary and our savior the lamb Jesus Christ, built directly on top of an altar to Jupiter, Juno, and Minerva. Who knows who is worshiped under there, how far down it goes from fifty-cent donations for a candle to a sacrificed bull to a sacrificed girl. Who knows who all may be listening to the prayers whispered there.

You pass through the labyrinth of twisty medieval streets and down the Venetian staircases that go all the way up the cliffs of the Carso, and spill yourself out into the grand Austro-Hungarian city squares with their straight lines and right angles, with their questionable taste in public fountains, with the gleaming white structures. Here is Triest, cut off to a sharp edge, and you can still feast at the Austrian restaurants and then sit outside, sweating out the sauerkraut and pork knuckle through your skin, belching out the heavy Austrian beers. The women who bake themselves on the cement slabs that pretend at being a seashore until they look as if they've stretched tight a thin layer of dark, leathered hide across their skeletons and pinned it behind their ears sit in cafés, drinking white wine and making gestures that look like expressions of pain. Here I order a Pimm's and ginger, which comes with an assortment of fruit haphazardly tossed into the glass. A large bowl of potato chips arrives, I suppose to replace the important salts that pour out of me in the late afternoon.

If I weren't distracted by my cocktail I would go onward, through Napoleon's Trieste and the roads he built to connect the city inward, or up to where it's spelled Trst, just over the ridge where the street signs are written in both Italian and Slovene. The buzzers of the city's apartment buildings are the passenger lists of castaways and the adrift, the names switching from Italian to German to Hungarian with that splattering of confetti accents dancing above the letters to French to Slavic.

And with one drink and one plate of chilled fish, all is right with the world. The whole expanse of time is playing itself out in one forgotten city. You can love all of it here, even the darkest moments, manifested in the Nazi memorabilia you find washed up in the antique stores' windows. Everyone here is as shockingly human and as fragile as you are, and you can love it all. You don't have to hold on so tight, you don't have to pursue anything, you can wait for the tide to bring back what it has taken from you. You can let it shift with the ever-crazy winds and love the whole world until it fills your rib cage and becomes so unbearable you need another drink to stifle it a little.

* * *

But we left Nora Barnacle up there somewhere, sitting on her luggage. As much as I write around that image of her alone in the dark, I can't gain access. Nora Barnacle is mostly blank space and dead air. We may sing along to Joyce's cover version of her, but the original has been lost. She was not dedicated to penning herself down, and what was once there, letters and ephemera, was destroyed or abandoned as they moved from place to place.

And humans are not good with blank space. We fill it, unconsciously, with bits of ourselves, with what we just assume would be there. Nora was the wife of a genius, coming from unfortunate circumstances, and so we the readers (and even her biographers) make our assumptions and then express surprise to discover exactly what we expected to find there. I put my hat on Nora's head and say, "Look how we share the same taste in hats!"

I keep filling Nora's blank space that night with my own thoughts and say, "Look at how much we think alike!"

I try to find a story about Nora that does not involve James, but it's not easy. There is no big stash of her letters and no journal. The infamously dirty letters Nora and James exchanged continue to exist only in James's hand—her half have been lost. We can only guess at what hers contained based on his responses. Her life is forever the unheard side of a telephone call.

But then not everyone wants to be remembered. Maybe my necromantic rites annoy the shit out of her, and she wishes I would stop trying to call her forth with my blood and my sword.

She's right not to trust me, one of the mistresses of my literary age, a woman who has found brilliant writers compelling enough to ignore the wife and children standing off there to the side, now trying to make nice with one of the wives of her literary age? It is little wonder that when I try to get inside her head, I find my way obscured. She has known women like me in her time. She has had to protect herself and her family from women like me in her time.

*　*　*

On my way home from cocktail hour one day, a gust of wind blows a bit of something or other into my eye, and in my inept attempts to get it out I scratch the thing across my cornea. Within a few hours the pain is intense, and even the dullest source of light is intolerable.

I worry about losing the eye. I also worry about not having health insurance here in Italy and making myself understood to a doctor, and so I self-treat. I walk around with my right hand clamped onto the side of my face for days. I can barely see well enough to read, and when I do read, I read the Internet. And of course the Internet tells me that I am going to lose the eye. It also tells me that when I rinsed my eye with tap water I probably introduced parasitic amoebae directly into my brain.

"You lost an eye?" a friend writes to me. "DON'T YOU THINK YOU ARE TAKING THIS JOYCE THING A LITTLE TOO FAR?"

*　*　*

My lover tells me on Skype he's coming to Italy to see me. He tells me this as I try to dig out the cork from a bottle of wine with a penknife while still holding onto my right eye to block out all light. I don't believe him. (I am scared to believe him.) I read his tarot cards. I am nowhere in his cards. My right eye weeps continuously as we talk, like a visible Freudian slip, revealing what I am trying to keep unconscious. 'Are you crying?" he asks me.

"No." Yes.

* * *

Here is something that happened to Nora that does not involve James: she lost two lovers. Of course the only reason we care about this is because of his brilliant novella *The Dead*, where a wife confesses to her husband that her true love is a dead man, but it did happen to her before James happened to her. Her paramours' deaths were just two shocks in a long line of shocks—in her childhood her family moved sever. times before her mother simply handed her over to Nora's grandmother to raise her, and then there was her father's continuous abandonment of the family in favor of alcohol. And then two suitors dead. One of typhoid, the other of tuberculosis.

How, after all that, was she not left with rocking, screaming, howling abandonment issues? Maybe she was, and this is simply one of the many things about Nora left unrecorded. We often interpret silence as strength, and what could be more silent or stronger than a solid Irish woman with a closed-mouth smile and no written record?

But it might explain why eventually James and Nora's life settled into a rather extreme codependency. One was not allowed to be without the other. James did not respond well to Nora's absences, and he sat and wrote down her experiences and memories and used them in his books. Nora stood by him through the drinking, through poverty, through his wandering eye and his sexual jealousy coupled with his insistence that she have an affair to help his writing. But maybe that is less codependency and more "being in a relationship," and it's only our self-help culture and constant assessment of relationships to keep them "healthy" and "honest" and "fulfilling" that keeps us from recognizing it for what it actually is. Likewise, maybe those abandonment issues are really just "being a human being," and now we can't help labeling all of our emotions as pathology.

* * *

After a week, my eye has healed. No more weeping, no more gripping half my face with my hand. And so I go to Rome to meet my lover, coming in from New York. Even on the train down I am not certain he will be there. There might be a last-minute text, a panicked apology that is high on emotion so I will not notice how vague it is on details. I spent the days before getting ready. Nails, hair, small refinements of my clothing. I want to make the visit perfect. Because then this time he might decide to stay rather than disappearing with a letter, a phone call from the airport. This time I can make him stay.

I am a very good mistress. I dress up, I perfume, I undress the moment he arrives. I do not ask him where he has been, with whom, what violations against my trust he has performed in my absence. I pretend, when he asks, that I have been faithful, both in head and in body, that I did not pick up what stray affections I could when they were made available, having become accustomed to scraps. I pretend that I am not open to the possibility of being swept away by some other at any time and at any place. I let him teach me things, I let him approve my dresses, I fuck him into splendor.

My lover has a secret wife that he is not telling me about, but part of me knows. As he lies next to me, I dream of calling him on the phone only to have another me answer, asking, "Why do you want to talk to him? He is a philanderer." In the morning I laugh at the oddness of the word, and I try to shake off what I somehow know.

I look over to see him in the bed, and feel him beside me.

His body cannot help but seek out mine in the night. If I pull away to readjust or to spare him my insomniac thrashing, he unconsciously crawls across the bed to find me. How can I possibly doubt what this is? As I fall back asleep, a thought worms its way to the front of my brain, all of my defenses against it lowered: maybe his sleeping body thinks that you are her.

But for the most part I allow my doubts and dreams to remain silent. In return for my silence I get Rome. I get prosecco and grappa. I get little golden shoes the color of medieval gilding, I get the history of the world whispered to me in sacred places. I get a plate of braised sheep intestines mixed in handmade pasta, the sexy funk of it filling the table between us. I get to watch him fearlessly dig into them. I get to laugh and watch him light up when I do. I get access to his body and to his marvelous brain. I get my own muse, as I write down his stories, his language, his history. I get fucked into splendor.

But this is how I know he has a secret wife: when I am with him, I have my mistress hat on, despite promises to myself that I will never put myself through this again, that I will never put a wife through this again. I feel like a mistress, and so, therefore. Ergo. If X, then Y.

I try not to notice how well the mistress hat fits me. How it suits me and so beautifully frames my face. I pretend I could be the wife, but I find that costume ill-fitting. And I wonder why, after all this time, these seem like the only two available options.

He travels back to Trieste with me and then quickly announces he must leave again, cut the planned three-week visit down to one. I don't know, I know, that he is going back to her. I drop the mistress act and reveal a hissing, furious little feral thing. Because he lies to me. He tells me I am the wife, and the distance between his fantasy and my reality is irreconcilable. The divide runs right through my brain, causing a dangerous schizophrenia. I hear whispers of truths I cannot possibly accept, I see visions of a ghost woman, and he tells me no, I am hallucinating, it is you, it is only you. I have never, you are, we are. We are.

On our way to the airport, there is a woman on the waterbus, sitting on the other side of the boat from her husband. He sits back, arm extended along the railing, looking for all the world as if he is in a state of dominion. She clutches her bag on her lap with both hands and, as the boat is in motion, never looks up from the floor.

Each time the boat pulls in to a stop, she half raises her body and looks over to her husband on the other side of the boat. "Here?" she seems to ask. He gives a kingly shake of his head and she sits back down, resuming her careful watch of her territory: her handbag, her seat, the rubber mat under her feet.

The boat pulls in for another stop, and the action repeats.

The lover and I disembark before they do, and as I watch the play they are putting on, it becomes clear: he, who will not sit by his nervous, disoriented wife, did not even give her the comfort of knowing where they are going.

The lover and I say our good-byes, and then I walk through the park, through the thick, electrical buzz of unseen cicadas, and make my way back home.

He leaves me at the train station with all my luggage, waiting for him to set up our home, to carry me across the threshold. And he? He has gone back to the one he cannot do without. For one week he has made me feel like treasure, and in one second he has revealed me to be nothing but trash.

I pull my shawl tighter and settle in for a long wait.

* * *

I have shared the biographers' disdain for the wife. I have condemned the lot of them as domestic, as made dull through overdoses of pregnancy hormones and dish soap. I have dismissed them as cozy as a cat sweater, as limiting and weighty.

And I have watched friends transform themselves into wives, start shutting down sections of their existence for the sake of the husband. I have seen them swap out their desires for their husbands' desires. I have seen them relinquish jobs, names, motherlands, and prospective motherhood because the desires of the wife were not the desires of the couple. I was raised by such a woman. The word *couple* itself brings to mind two people sewn together with twine, neither able to move in any direction without dragging along the other. I have seen the worst of wifedom and on that basis I have condemned the entire pursuit.

There was splendor in the early days of Nora and James. What she relinquished to her husband was any sense of stability, and in return she got adventure. Travel. Genius. Certainly a chambermaid from West Ireland with no specific ambitions would not have achieved such things on her own.

But adventure comes with its twin, fear. Their material situation swung wildly as James relied on patrons for their well-being. Landlords, discovering they were not legally married, evicted them. They shuffled from country to country. Their daughter's mind was unstable, too, and she began to throw furniture at her mother and start fires. And what had once been a passionate life together burned itself out. The marriage became celibate, after such a dirty start.

The roles they played to each other, for each other, became fixed. Nora as wife, running a household on the infuriatingly little money James brought in. James as husband, out with mates at the bar until the wee hours. And so then also James as Drunk and Nora as Scold. By all reports James was a happy drunk, slipping into the neck of a wine bottle and coming out singing. But when someone lays claim to the position of Drunk, the only role left is that of Scold. The only one who doesn't see what's funny about their spouse lying prone and unmovable on the floor yet again, or their spouse being carried unconscious home on someone's back yet again.

We don't like to admit it, but we are shaped by our interactions with our environment. The rock-solid self we believe in turns out to be vulnerable to erosion. And so after years of someone going after you in the same way, you hold your body differently; reactions become reflexes. Your pose hardens. And sometimes, after long enough, you find your body doesn't bend back the other way anymore.

Living with the winds of Trieste is a bit like living with a drunk, from what I remember of my time in that particular role. Windows and doors bang with no warning. Occasionally you are knocked into a wall. When you come home, nothing will be where you left it.

But you cannot just seal off the windows: the air gets thick and stale, and you miss the chaos. It has become familiar. So you try to manage it instead. You are strategic in your opening and closing of doors and windows. You provide buffers to muffle any bangs. You never give your opponent a direct line of attack. You silently pick up the objects left in disarray, saving real resistance for a real gale.

One night in Trieste I was awakened by cacophony. My shutters, the shutters of the entire building and the building next door, had all come loose in the wind and were clattering madly, banging themselves against the outer walls. When I reached the window, lightning struck the sea right in front of me, and I felt the attack of thunder bodily. I cowered until I recovered my breath, then stood back up at the window, reaching for the shutters and some rope to secure them. There was a wall of water—it did not resemble rain in the slightest, moving as it did horizontally—and the trees appeared to be missing. But no, they were just displaced. They were all somehow parallel to the ground, bent over as if they were humans being dragged by their hair.

I finally tied the shutters closed, watching others struggle with the same task, and heard that the shutters at the other end of my apartment had now come loose. I crawled back into bed, my hands clamped over my ears, terrified in a nonspecific way and yet somehow able to easily fall back asleep. Because for years this state had been perfectly normal.

* * *

I wish I were a man. If I were I would be Richard Burton; but, being only a woman, I would be Richard Burton's wife.

LETTER FROM ISABEL BURTON TO HER FAMILY

The longer I stay in Trieste, the more I am pulled, physically and figuratively, up to the Carso where the Burtons lived.

Trieste was an unlikely home for Richard Francis Burton and an even more unlikely location for his deathbed. Here was the great man, after a life of adventure and exploring, of sex and mysticism, a man who fluently spoke twenty-nine languages and named mountains, dying in a conservative Austro-Hungarian outpost while holding down a government job as a consul. And here was his Catholic wife Isabel, performing last rites on his silent, unprotesting, very un-Catholic body to try to ensure their afterlife reunion, like it's all just a big magic trick that requires a little sleight-of-hand with God. (And later, here was his wife tossing his final manuscript into the fire, a manuscript that was rumored to be the greatest accomplishment of Burton's tremendous career, thus allowing her name to be cursed by Burton scholars and readers for generations, even to this day.)

Trieste held little interest for Burton, but when you spend your life making sure everyone knows you are smarter and better than they are, and you work in government, you will end your days in a place like this, bored and cramped. For just about anyone else, the sea, the opera, the food, the train system into the continent, and the seaport out to North Africa would have been heaven. But not for a man who feels more natural in disguise, on a camel, riding into certain death and laughing his way out of it.

As much as Trieste bored him and he repeatedly applied for leaves of absence from his post, as much as it confined him like a smaller man's jacket, Richard Francis Burton did his most important work here. In a real house with real furniture, living with a wife and not a servant/lover, in a city where he held down a regular job, he translated the *Kama Sutra* and *Arabian Nights*. Here he brought the East to the West, and the West called it obscene. And then bought every single copy.

Isabel was a different matter altogether. She was not a feral made domestic, she was a domestic who managed to unearth dormant feral genes. A good and proper member of the penniless aristocracy—one of the nineteenth-century families who were passed down good names and titles and family houses and that is it—she would have had the job of restocking the family fortunes with a good marriage. Her inheritance, plus her good looks and her being a delight by all reports, was enough to draw a great number of suitors. Men flocked to her, but the men bored her. She wanted adventure, and being "only a woman," she decided the only way to get it was through an adventurous husband.

I understand the impulse to be Richard Burton. Who would not want to be that brave, that bold? Who wouldn't want to be able to take a spear through the face while on an expedition in Somalia, and then have the pride to sit scar-out for every portrait that followed? Who wouldn't want to let their British colleagues drink their gin and tell the same boring stories for the nth time while you learn the native language and all its corresponding dialects, which you would then use to seduce the local ladyfolk?

But I also understand the impulse to be the wife of Richard Burton—to marry adventure and not have to embody it. To follow with the luggage once the housing has already been set up. To have someone who speaks the language and can take care of the day-to-day interactions in the foreign land, someone who leads your camel after he's decided the route. It's much easier to be brave with someone else drawing the map.

Which is not to discount Isabel's bravery. She rode into malaria and tribal conflict and sleeping rough like the best of them, and there were not many women of her time who would have been up for it. Being married to Richard Burton means all of your bravery is in the form of reaction, not action. That has its downside, like feeling that all of your life you are sitting on a small wheeled thing, being pulled by your husband with a bit of string. But Isabel's capacity for trust and receptivity must have been enormous. And that makes her more of a mystery to me than Richard.

And let's not forget: facing down spinsterhood for the satisfaction of demands is its own kind of bravery.

* * *

The heat of Trieste is shocking and thick. "It is not usually this hot," Massimo tells me. I am eating spaghetti with clams, we are right on the water, the sun has left the sky, and yet the heat still radiates from the ground, from our bodies, even the incandescent light bulb above us seems to beat down an intolerable heat.

I sweat like a purification ritual. I fill myself with wine and my body just turns it into sugar. I cannot get drunk here. A bottle, a second bottle goes down, and instantly comes out of my skin and seals my dress to my body. I am enjoying it after the damp, clammy German spring I just endured. I am enjoying the surrender. I am enjoying being a body.

I tell Massimo of being awakened by the dreaded windstorm, and he tells me it is even worse in the winter. "It's like all the air of Central Europe is funneled down and has to exit the continent through this tiny space." Each season's wind has its own name and its own personality. I'm told to check wind forecasts before walking along the shore, lest I be picked up and carried off to sea. As he drives me home he talks of the history of port wine and its long journeys over the Atlantic. I can't help it, after all of my reading I am wondering what it would be like to be married to him, even though his sexuality is an androgynous mystery. What worlds would he open up, like Richard did for Isabel, like James did for Nora? He is a translator gifted in languages, he knows about wine and sea travel. I sit in the passenger seat and let his voice make pictures in my head.

Have I always done this, treated men like doors rather than partners? Seeing them for what kind of world they can take me out into, rather than their own particular qualities? This flattens out the men I love, it is ceaselessly unfair. And yet I find myself incapable of stopping. I love my lover, but every time I meet a new man I construct elaborate fantasies about joining his traveling party, all the wonderful new territories he could take me to.

I am, I remind myself, here in Trieste under my own steam, with train fare that came from my earnings, after I had the idea to do it. I drew the map to this marvelous place, and I led my own camel.

But where is my Isabel, I wonder. To follow with the luggage and be a companion in foreign lands. Maybe, a tiny voice whispers, she'll show up when you finally admit to being Richard Francis Burton.

There is something very "I don't know, what do you want to do" about Trieste. It is right on the border between Italy and Slovenia, a stone's throw from Croatia, specifically the part that used to be Italy. Or whatever this mass was called. I keep forgetting, as I stare at the maps trying to get the timeline straight in my head, how young Italy the nation is. It's easy for an American to think of nations as linear, progressing steadily onward, perhaps expanding but never shrinking. Europeans are more accustomed to shifting borders, to a constantly renewed and tinkered-with cartography, as new lines are drawn and others erased, and as chunks of larger selves subdivide again and again. This land mass all used to be part of the same hulk, back when it was Austro-Hungarian.

But of course it was also Venetian for a while. British for a while. Trieste was squabbled over by Yugoslavia and the Soviet Union for a while. Roman in the way back. It was occupied by Americans. Twice it was a free port, but it flinched at the responsibilities of freedom and latched itself to whichever suitor came next. In this last case it was Italy, and so now it is Italian.

There are no monuments to the great Triestine resistance, when men picked up their weapons and said, "No more. This is who we are, we will not stand for this occupation." There are people in this city today who went through those long periods of disorientation, when official languages and currencies and flags were switched over again and again. Some had to flee to stay within their preferred borders, but most just shrugged and exchanged their money and adjusted their calendars to the new national holidays.

It can't be much different from being a wife in Nora's times, in Isabel's times, having little say in how things go, resigning oneself to the latest circumstances. One stays out of loyalty and devotion and the excitement of uncertainty, and probably not a little fear about what it would be like to reject these local circumstances to wander across the border. The external structures of your life may be chaos, but at least the smallest unit you exist in—the shop where you get groceries, the bed you wake up in—remains stable.

Not that it wasn't done, sometimes. Nora was a contemporary of Coco Chanel. Isabel coincided with Gertrude Bell. But even though it happened sometimes, being an individual and a woman at the same time, it just *wasn't done*, and that dissuaded most.

I wonder who was plagued with what-ifs. Isabel never looked back. (Her instructions to herself on her wedding day are extensive and detailed, but her final, seventeenth, directive stands out: "Keep everything going and let nothing ever be at a standstill: nothing would weary him like stagnation.") We will never know what doubts played their way through Nora's brain. She did run off once, after a long period of dealing with James's heavy drinking and financial instability. She did not stay away long.

It's doubtful Trieste had many regrets, watching as it did, up close, the second, horrific half of Yugoslavia's twentieth century.

A great hulking trapezoid squats heavily on the ridge above Trieste, visible all the way to the Slovenian border. At night it is dramatically lit from below, shooting its menacing rays into space. The first time I saw it, my reflexive thought was *Oh, that must be where they sacrifice virgins to the gods of the underworld.* It looks evil.

"Oh that?" Massimo glanced over his shoulder at the structure and was not instantly transformed into a hell hound, brimstone smoking out of his wet muzzle. "It is a monument to the Virgin Mary, built to remind the godless communists of Yugoslavia what they were missing."

"It doesn't look . . . compassionate."

"No, it's a little ominous, isn't it? I don't know what they were thinking."

* * *

The wife: revealed. The lover slips her name, I google until I find her, and then I fire off an e-mail to her to confirm. She writes back. And then again. And again and again. Every day when I wake up, a little bouquet of missives from the wife. I know everything about her now, she's revealing her soft underbelly in the hopes that I'll take pity and retreat. I hold back my own information, I reveal only the smallest bits. Mostly, though, I lie.

It is a blessing when the apartment wifi shorts out. I am allowed to wake up to birdsong (the never-ceasing shrieking of seagulls) and a solitary cup of tea, rather than her voice her text her territorial pissings coming though my laptop.

But I need an Internet connection to file my work, so here I am at the Trieste shopping mall, sitting at the fountain as children hopped up on colored sugar run around me in circles. Someone is auditioning young women here for a beauty contest, the Miss Topolini. Last year's contestants are plastered on giant signs, posing in swimsuits with hands on their hips and a slight lurch, giving their best catalog with beauty-queen smiles. Lithe girls just out of acne and braces line up in identical black bikinis between the discount shoe store and a Gap knockoff, hoping to be chosen, hoping to be taken away from this notch in Italy's Adriatic armpit, this city that no one remembers. Maybe a photographer will see them in their sash and tiara, see beyond the awkward cheesiness of it all, and put them in *Vogue*. Take them to Paris or Milan. Which is another way to be a wife, I guess: utilizing your distinctly female inventory and allowing yourself to be steered by men.

My lover was in this city for only two days, and yet he has already taken it away from me. The café I went to almost every day before his arrival is now the café where we went. My bed is now our bed. My skee-ball machine at the shopping mall arcade is now his skee-ball machine at the shopping mall arcade, seeing how he beat me on it three rounds in a row. I must take this city back from him, now that I know about her. Now that I know the we, the us, was not a proper noun, just a random grouping. It is still very hot outside, and so I think I will start my reclamation project with the skee-ball machine.

I pump in tokens and get into my zen skee-ball head space. Pick up a ball, roll with the precise swing of muscle memory toward the 50, hear the delicious hum as it makes its way up the ramp, don't even look up to see where it lands before reaching down for another. Repeat, repeat, repeat. At least be grateful the wifi is out so you can't stalk Hera's online presence late at night. Repeat, repeat, repeat. Don't think about his promise to return next month or the fact that he never lives up to his promises. Repeat, repeat, repeat. I think later we can do this with those cocktails you guys had. Refill your tokens at the machine and then repeat, repeat, repeat.

Eventually James came back for his Nora at that little park. It was morning when he rejoined her. She laughed or sighed or yelled or cried or showed no reaction at all. Either she regretted traveling halfway across Europe with this irresponsible man or she thought, *I knew he'd come back for me.* Either she recognized that their arrival set up a pattern that would repeat through their relationship, or she did not.

They walked off into the rising sun to set up a home in their new lodgings.

* * *

It would be nice if things in real life ended like that, on an uplift.

* * *

I walk to a town named Prosecco for obvious reasons, taking Napoleon's road. It's high up on the Carso, the limestone plateau that surrounds this whole area. The road begins with an old inn, left to go to ruin in the trees, an old retreat of the Burtons. It is vacant, if you don't count the arboreal life that has taken up occupation inside. As I walk to my destination of more pasta, more wine, I entertain the fantasy of buying the inn, settling in Trieste, naming it after the great traveler himself. Maybe if I settle I can do my own great work. Maybe I can put an ad on Craigslist, Looking for a Man to Be My Wife.

When I return to the apartment, I have just enough time to shower and dress, as the great writer Claudio Magris is picking me up. He calls, he's here, where am I? I race down, and there he is in his car, with a face that looks carved out of the Trieste cliffs, as if designed by God specifically for the formidable bust that will mark his passing and take its rightful place next to Svevo, Joyce, Saba, and all of the other Triestine husbands in the city park.

"I will make us grapefruit juice, and we will talk," he tells me.

His bookshelves reflect the list of conquerors of Trieste, books in Italian, books in Croatian, in Slovenian, in German, in French. There is only one American author on his shelves, and in a moment that I have to chalk up to one of the universe's idiot pranks, I see it is written by the first married man with whom I fell in love. I move away quickly as if it had grown fangs and snapped at me, and settle into a chair across the room.

Magris returns with the grapefruit juice. We can sit near the window as the sun has dropped its All Seeing Eye of God routine, and everything blooms rosy in the city as we talk. "Trieste has become boring," Magris tells me, and you can feel it in the quiet of the evening. It's the boringness of a morning spent in bed with a cup of tea and a book you're not entirely engaged with. The boredom of a dinner with someone you love spent in shared silence. The boredom of a long walk to a place you know well, with a plentiful supply of water and a pocket full of almonds. It is the boredom of adequacy.

"Thank god for the boredom," he says after a pause. Since his birth in the late 1930s, Magris's time in Trieste has seen fascism, Nazism, and communism. It's seen genocide and atrocity, nationalism and civil war. It stood by as its neighbor Yugoslavia tore itself into bits. Did Trieste feel it when its former territory in Dalmatia began to bleed, like a cramp in a ghost limb? Or did it shrug and turn the page like most of the rest of Europe? Trieste saw greatness too, and genius, but it traded it in for a quiet life in the country.

We move from his apartment to his second favorite restaurant. His favorite is closed for the summer, the owners off on a retreat of their own. He is ordering for me, and I am filling myself on his choices: calamari, the inevitable spaghetti with clams, panna cotta, and a white wine that despite the ice bucket hits a temperature equilibrium with the heavy night air the second it's poured into our glasses. My needs are met. I am bored. It is glorious.

It is my last night in Trieste, and the moon is over the sea and there is nothing I could possibly need. And yet I want. I realize my Richard Burton Inn is a misguided tribute. A woman who stops her wandering to host the wanderings of others? What a dismal idea.

Magris drives me home in silence, and I just want to hang out the window, worshiping the waning moon, the smell of the sea, all salt and murk and hidden intentions. I would slay myself on the altar of boredom if given the chance. Which is why I am mostly relieved to be greeted at my apartment by my already packed suitcase, and I reach into my pocket for the twenty-eighth time to reassure myself the bus ticket to Ljubljana is still there.

Sarajevo / Rebecca West

I wasn't sure, all those years ago on the train from Austria to Slovenia, what the procedure was exactly. My train compartment was empty, so there was no one to mimic, no one who spoke the language and knew what was going on whose actions I could simply duplicate. That is of course the easiest way to figure out local customs, just do what everyone else is doing. Except for in Russia. When in Russia, you should generally do the exact opposite of what everyone else is doing.

But in my quiet compartment, following a last-minute *well, I'm in Austria and Slovenia is right there* kind of whim, I had panicked myself into stasis. I had no idea of Slovenia, no inner image, no reference points at all. Except war and stuff, news reports during the breakup of Yugoslavia. But I think that was Bosnia and Croatia, I can't remember anything ever being said about Slovenia. Train conductors kept poking their heads in, and I would jerk upright and present them my passport, but no one ever wanted my passport. They would look at me with that "what is wrong with you" cock of the head and then swiftly disappear without a word. I kept it out and readily available anyway. I didn't know you could travel freely between Austria and Slovenia or that it was part of the EU. Upon arrival I would race to the ATM to withdraw money in the local currency, only to discover the local currency was the euro. But before that, in my train car, instead of relaxing and enjoying the autumnal color blurring outside my window, I sat alert, passport gripped in my hands, ever ready to identify myself and never catching on that no one cared.

But then something in my periphery distracted me from my vigilance. As we crossed from Austria into Slovenia, a massive statue erupted from the hillside unexpectedly. A man, sword held aloft, staring from Slovenia back across the Austrian frontier. "We are sick of your empire-building bullshit," the statue seemed to be saying. "Don't even fucking think about it." Where on earth was I going?

* * *

That week-long stay in Slovenia was my first dipped toe in the Balkans, and I wanted desperately to go back. The alluring Ljubljana, with its venomous secrets, called to me, despite my inability to ever pronounce it properly. The original plan for my return was to follow Rebecca West's trip through Yugoslavia. She had been sent on assignment by the *Atlantic* and would produce the massive thousand-plus-page 1944 travelogue / history / journalism / political science / philosophical quandary *Black Lamb and Grey Falcon*. In six weeks she traveled through every major city, every site of historical significance, every village that contained an architectural marvel. It was the first time anyone from Western Europe had cared much about the region, and so I guess she decided she needed to be comprehensive. Following in West's footsteps while rereading her tome seemed like a good crash course.

That plan quickly fell apart. Both Croatia and Montenegro had in the past years recovered from being war-torn, postcommunist dead zones and were now beach getaways, with all of the inflated peak-season hotel prices that that role suggests. Travel infrastructure between the splintered states was not exactly a top priority for any of the governments, and so I was looking at day-long trips just to get from one city to another. Not to mention that West had traveling companions, a local fixer, someone to carry her luggage, a husband to keep her company, and her hotel bills paid. My pilgrimage was going to be self-funded and self-guided. I totaled up the projected expenses, balked, and decided to simply pick a few places on her itinerary and set up longer stays in Ljubljana, Belgrade, and Sarajevo.

Besides, West's whirlwind tour seemed to have her in each place for only a day or two, at a few places even less. I am less easily uprooted and replanted. I am a slow traveler, and I do not mean that in a pretentious Slow Food kind of way, suggesting that I savor experiences more deeply and more thoroughly than the normal traveler. I mean it takes me ages to recover from each journey and ages to absorb a new vista. If I spent only two days in Belgrade, 80 percent of that would be spent in bed, trying to convince myself to put on my shoes and go out the door, and chastising myself harshly when that did not work.

West is a robust traveler. I am really not. Adjustments had to be made.

When West showed up in 1937, Europe had barely recovered from the First World War, and it was beginning to become clear that things were about to spiral out again. West, a journalist, critic, and novelist, wanted to understand how such a neglected, obscure place could have been responsible for the potential annihilation of Europe. As did her mostly American and British audience, many of whom probably first heard the name Sarajevo when the city was being indicted for starting the war to end all wars. "Since there proceeds steadily from the southeastern corner of Europe a stream of events which are a danger to me, which indeed for years threatened my safety and deprived me forever of many benefits, that is to say I know nothing of my own destiny," she wrote in her introduction. If the act of one man could ripple out to cause widespread devastation, it might be important to understand the context that man came from.

We pin the beginning of World War I at the assassination of Franz Ferdinand by a Serb in Sarajevo, instead of perhaps the more appropriate place: the extended deprivation of oxygen suffered by German leader Kaiser Wilhelm during his birth. That is to say, in high school history class I was taught like everyone was taught that one crazed man started a war that killed millions, rather than what should have been taught, that your government has no problem throwing your body into a fiery hellscape when it gets bored and pissy.

Why would anyone care about the far reaches of the Other Europe unless it somehow affected their daily lives back in the civilized bits? A bluestocking and socialist, West seemed like the perfect writer to take on the obscure region. She had led a marginalized existence for most of her life—first because of poverty, then due to her family's move to Scotland, then just by being a woman in intellectual society, and finally for being an unwed mother. She should understand what it is like to be prejudged, what it was like to be spoken for rather than being able to speak for oneself.

She would never take the conservative view, that Gavrilo Princip, a poor radical anarchist, was to blame for all that followed his assassination of the presumptive heir to the Austro-Hungarian Empire. She understood not only how the oppressed were forced into acts of extreme violence but also how those acts were sometimes necessary. *Black Lamb and Grey Falcon* is almost pro-assassination with the amount of compassion she heaps on top of Princip and his co-conspirators. West is at her best as she recounts a long line of assassinations and regicides—Yugoslavia has had all kinds of tyrannical leaders and crazed conspirators plotting revenge. West excites at the smell of blood. Or maybe she can sympathize with those who use their force of will to change the direction of their own story.

Black Lamb and Grey Falcon is indeed a masterpiece, and certainly it contains the best writing of West's career. Her depiction of the assassination of Franz Ferdinand is part thriller, part slapstick. It remains perhaps the greatest account of that oft-relayed event. She does not pretend not to know why a whole region may have wanted the heir to an empire dead, and she does not pretend that imperial forces are there to help their conquered lands. History may be written by the winners, but at least West's history roots for the underdog.

But reading this material now is a very different act from reading the book in the 1940s. Sarajevo is no longer a city of mystery, nor are the names Belgrade, Croatia, Montenegro, Kosovo strange to our ear. West had empty spaces to work with — her readers were coming to her book with fewer ideas about the region, other than that thing that the West does to the East, imagining that darker impulses and darker blood come with the darker skin and hair. But they didn't have the very specific images from news reports of the atrocities committed in the 1990s or the stories of mass rape and ethnic cleansing cluttering up their heads. They had not already constructed elaborate theories to explain how something like that war happens in a civilized age.

And so Rebecca West, twenty years or so after the start of World War I, took a six-week trip through Yugoslavia. And I, twenty years or so after the Balkan Wars, am spending a month in the former Yugoslavia. She filled a thousand pages with her observations and analysis. I'm looking to fill one chapter. Lord knows I'm hardly going to be that guy, the one who goes to the former Yugoslavia to "understand" the region and offer some sort of psychotic explanation to an American audience for the violence and hatred he is hoping to find there so that he can make his name. I have read enough on the subject to be familiar with the oft-trotted-out quip about "ancient hatreds." I heard someone on the BBC saying that "martyrdom is part of the Serbian psyche." There are all sorts of horrible things we tell ourselves about people we find embarrassing, in order to separate them out, to identify them as Other, to deny any similarities, any familiar impulses, any shared blood. To explain why our society would never crumble so, and while we are certainly quick to declare war, it's not like *that*, never for such nonsensical reasons. We keep our bloodthirsty impulses under the control of our rational brains.

After centuries of neglect by the outside world, now there are dozens of experts from England, Western Europe, America, who flooded into the area to gawk, to investigate, and then to fill books with their explanations of what went wrong. Once the fighting was over, of course. Very few people gave a shit when the war was happening. I am acutely aware of my need not to be that person, the civilized touring through the uncivilized. The expert who reduces the chaos to something understandable. I don't want to tell anyone what they want to hear, that this is an anomaly, that there is just something about this region that breeds violence and discord. But neither can one just be a tourist, out hiking in the until-recently-laced-with-mines mountains, using cheap deregulated European airlines to distract me from my existential boredom. I can't just go for the cheap beer and meat pastries, the *New York Times*–approved Belgrade nightclubs and sex with manly Balkan men. What role that leaves for me, though, I'm not entirely sure.

* * *

Oddly, West bypassed Slovenia almost entirely on her tour of Yugoslavia. Ljubljana gets the briefest of mentions, and she heads straight through the country to get to Croatia. But I want to linger in Ljubljana, as this city is my Central European trading post, the perfect resting spot for a weary English-speaking traveler. One can stock up on English-language books in the beautiful bookstores; there is plum brandy and a large central market with a vending machine that doles out unpasteurized farm-fresh milk for your morning coffee. The only words I ever retain in Slovene are the words for "cheese pastry, please." Within minutes of stashing my luggage at my sublet, I am off to my favorite bakery to trot out my entire vocabulary.

Ljubljana is a perfect little fairy-tale jewel box. The directions to the apartment where I'm staying include "turn right at the castle," and the first time I visited the city it was wrapped in a dreamy fog. Ljubljana has taken St. George and the Dragon as its foundational myth, but it seems to have sided with the dragon rather than the saint. Dragons line the bridges; they fly on the city crest. The art museum has a mischievous room of relics, little vials of blood, chipped-off bits of bone, all presented wrapped in gold and jewels. As soon as I slip over the border, there are no more tranquil deer nibbling on branches, sipping water from a sun-dappled brook. I see only predators, never prey. Fox, hawks, cats, falcons.

The city is so storybook, so tightly contained, so completely founded in a mythological realm and not in our own, that it is hard to imagine war ever happened here. It bears no scars, there are no wayward bullet holes, no uncleared rubble. Perhaps that is why West ignored it: it is so obviously living out a different storyline than the rest of the region, perhaps even the rest of the world. One cannot make it fit. Even during the smash-up of Yugoslavia, Slovenia slipped out quietly, only a few dozen people killed during what might as well have been heated arguments in comparison to what happened to the rest of the countries. Ljubljana did not get involved in the struggles of its brothers and sisters; it sat in its Neptune haze, wondering what happened here, forgetting that something did.

I cannot stay here long; it is only a brief stop on my way deeper into the region for provisions and a frivolous hat. (Made of rabbit fur. Even the milliners are predatory here, their tight smiles concealing shining sharp teeth.) The last morning I am running late for my nine-hour train to Belgrade. I am less than a mile from the station, but I fear I won't make it dragging my suitcase behind me. (Damn Rebecca and her hotel porters.) I stop a cab and ask the driver to take me to the station. He looks at me queerly. "It is close. You should walk." He won't let me into the backseat. I want to stomp my feet, I want to yell, "I will give you all of my money," but I pick up my belongings in a huff and speed on to the station, where the train is blessedly delayed. Perhaps the train forgot where it was going and wandered off for a bit in the fog.

* * *

The day before I leave for Belgrade, I watch an old episode of *Prime Suspect* on my laptop. An innocent (angelically blond, blue-eyed, rosy-cheeked) Bosnian Muslim girl has been found tortured and murdered in London, and of course a Serb, a former officer in the army, is a suspect. The good British detective, played by Helen Mirren, goes to Bosnia to uncover evidence of a massacre, but these foolish Bosnians, they will not speak with her, they refuse to cooperate, they are too frightened of reprisals. The detective rants in frustration. Don't they know this is in their best interest? Why must they be so dull-witted?

Another Bosnian Muslim girl is murdered before they can bring the killer to justice, a man who also engineered the deaths of dozens during the Yugoslav War. The female detective speaks of ancient hatreds, of ethnic tensions. The Serbians are incomprehensible—they are all animal, no intellect, running on instinct and an unstoppable thirst for blood.

It is silly. The man, the killer, the Serb, he is cold and charming; they uncover the bodies of his victims, they bring closure. The British, I mean. They civilize the uncivil and bring meaning to the meaningless. They explain the Yugoslav War to an English audience in a way the English audience can understand. And the English audience nods and never thinks to themselves, *Strange, how that explanation is exactly what we wanted it to be. Our society, so civilized, so intellectual, would never come apart like that.* The chaos has been controlled by the cool intellect of the West. They sleep soundly.

* * *

A man on my train to Belgrade is so obviously German, it is like he is holding a sign above his head, declaring it in flashing lights. From the socks with sandals to the cargo shorts to the neatly parted blond hair, he is Deutsch. He helps me with my luggage, as well as the luggage of every other woman in our compartment. He sits down and pulls a giant pretzel out of his bag, just in case anyone was in doubt of his origins. I try not to stare, but I am happy he is there. If things get too out of order, he will rein them back in. Alas, he leaves the train before Belgrade, and an unfamiliar case of the nerves sets in when he goes.

Rebecca West pauses for a moment in her writing and considers: every person of a certain age here in Yugoslavia has seen horrors. First in the Balkan Wars against the Ottoman Empire, and then in World War I. She writes, "All the Yugoslavs over forty must have taken part in a military campaign of the most appalling nature, and all adults who were below that age had undergone as boys privations and dangers such as never threatened French or English or German children." And not all of those horrors were the horrors of victimhood; some of them originated here. She wonders, when she looks around her, which of these seemingly normal folk busy in their daily lives had a part to play in the violence.

From the moment I disembark, I am echoing Rebecca's question. I step off the train and immediately go rigid. The difference between my relaxed, blissful state in Slovenia and my state in Serbia is marked. My hand tightens around the handle of my suitcase, I am holding on to the strap of my backpack. I am almost expecting the men in the station to gather around me and forcibly remove my belongings. I am not like this, this is not how I am, and there's nothing physically different about this train station, it looks like all train stations, but I can't shake it. When a man sneers at me, which is a thing that happens all over the world, here in this train station I sneer back and think darkly, *I know what you did, motherfucker.*

Too many news reports about Serbs being the aggressors, too many images from the siege of Sarajevo, too many statistics about mass rape used as a weapon, about ethnic cleansing, about ancient hatreds, too many shots of Milosevic's evil smug face—it has all seeped into my unconscious, and when I look around me I see only monsters.

It's an unfair trick of the brain, and I try to fight it. It is the reaction some Americans have when they first come to Germany. A particularly confused American man sat across from me on a beautiful spring day at a Berlin sidewalk café, little cakes and cups of milchkaffee between us, spewing nothing but hatred for the people around him. "Don't you wonder, whenever you see an old man on the street?"

"What's that?"

"What he was doing during the war. We're still surrounded by Nazis. And all these people," he said as he looked around, "they're the children of Nazis."

I had judged this man in that moment, despite the fact that

it is understandable, given how much of the story of our history revolves around the idea of the German as the Bad Guy, the Worst of All Possible. The only time the German accent showed up in our movies was when it was coming out of the mouths of men dressed as Nazis, and now that accent is all around us. Our brain jumps to the association, it is often the only one we have.

I judged the American for not being able to stand back from that, for his inability to recognize what a cruel assumption he was making. We all occupy space on top of one atrocity or another, blood has coated every square inch of this earth. We can never live somewhere pure, where no one ever died horrifically simply because something about their identity made them suspicious. The fact that the atrocities we shared in our American bloodlines—slavery, the ethnic cleansing of our own indigenous people—happened further back does not mean we are any less culpable. Or they are any more so.

If I ever had to account for the particular evils in my genetic code, the trial would last for centuries. I have slave owners, Protestant invaders of Ireland, and Vikings in my family tree. I have Cromwell loyalists. The unattended colonial nightmares of the British part of my family alone could push the trial into the next millennium. All of the people who had to die to guarantee my existence—if they could stand to give testimony, I couldn't stand the reckoning.

Understanding the violence of our history does not mean we refuse to condemn atrocity when we see it because we resign ourselves to its everywhere existence. Contemporary Hungary is again trying to deny its involvement in the Holocaust—oh well, evil resides all around us, let's get a hamburger. But fixating on one group, identifying them as the Bogeyman of the Twentieth Century, allows anyone who fails to top their monstrosity a bit of a free pass. It lets Hungary deny its involvement: what does it really matter, we've already dealt with the German source and we're so very tired of thinking about it all. It also lets our country continue to terrorize other nations with our drone campaigns, assist in the takedown of popularly elected foreign governments, invade countries and lie to justify it. It's not like we are *Nazis*, let's get some perspective. We benefit greatly from pointing our fingers, and until we understand that, we will keep deflecting.

And blanket labeling also blankets variation, nuance, any sense of how such a situation is created; it numbs our understanding of how nations fall apart, how crowds fall under the sway of madmen, how situations are created and develop. Once you use the word *evil*, it blots out context. Evil doesn't need to be understood, it just drops into our world from another dimension. It also allows it to be an "over there" problem.

I know all of this intellectually, so why in Belgrade do I find myself doing a wicked math? I subtract twenty years from everyone around me and picture them with blood on their hands. I do not see people, I see Serbs. My first thought when a man of a certain age begins to talk to me is *What did* you *do during the war?* It is ungenerous, and I am ashamed of my knee-jerk response, but I seem incapable of halting it.

I try to determine what the difference is. I feel unsafe. Where Slovenia was kind of sexy in its threat of violence, Belgrade is brutal. There is no sleekness, no elegance to its predation: it is men in large groups, leering, and large dogs with thick jaws, all roaming free in packs. West romanticized the manliness of the Serbian male, going on and on about how his physicality and arrogant potency made her feel like a real woman, not like those British men who traded in their cocks for extra brain space. But turning someone into a fetish is just as much an act of othering as turning him into a bogeyman.

I notice as I walk through the streets after dropping off my bags at the apartment that I do not see any women. Not in the cafés, not on the sidewalk, not in the grocery store. It's all men. Men and dogs and walled-off houses and blocks of concrete. "Real" men do not make me feel like a real woman, they make me feel like prey. And I group them that way, all of these individuals, under the heading "Men, Menacing." I feel menaced. I buy a bottle of vodka and a watermelon, and I return to my apartment.

* * *

By the time Rebecca West wrote *Black Lamb and Grey Falcon* she was a respected intellectual, a role she had worked incredibly hard for. As soon as she reached adulthood she had begun publishing thousands and thousands of pages of fiction and journalism and criticism, publishing in feminist publications and carefully managing her contacts and publishing credits to grow her career and influence. She made a surgical strike against Henry James just as he was being seen as old-fashioned, in a way that was sure to start arguments in review sections and in salons. If she were writing today, we would call her guilty of intellectual linkbait. If she were writing today, she would be writing for *n+1*.

"That is the thing about Rebecca West," a publishing friend e-mails. "She was not a genius but talented, too much ambition at the same time as not enough ambition." Perhaps just ambition for the wrong thing: attention rather than revolution. Ambition for attention means playing by certain rules, it means being an iconoclast in pre-approved ways.

It's unclear whether women like Rebecca West wear their ambitions awkwardly or whether we are still uncomfortable with ambitious women. I am uncomfortable with ambitious Rebecca West simply because her profligacy, in the end, seems to add up to so little. A few memorable quips, a handful of brilliantly insightful essays, and then her greatest moment, *Black*

Lamb. Which itself suffers from an excess of profligacy, needing to be about half the size it is. I edit it as I read through it, wishing she had less of the certainty that a specific type of Edwardian British brain overflows with, that whole "I have been around a particular culture for a few weeks and now I understand it fully despite not speaking the language, here is how it works" thing.

But then how to get this job, sent out by the *Atlantic* to Yugoslavia with hotel bills paid for and the logistics kindly worked out by someone else, unless what you have learned to do in your career is to tell the stories the way the people in power want them to be told? There is a time and place to celebrate true radicals, but that time and place comes mostly after they are dead. Magazines and newspapers still do this to their women writers, preferring to hire women who tell us that motherhood is a joy, educated women are more likely to die alone, et cetera. If you want to speak to a big audience and your own platform seems to draw little attention, before you go on someone else's stage you are going to have to clear your comments with the men who built it.

If I were editing *Black Lamb*, I would ask Rebecca to question her assumptions. I would ask her to include doubt. I would cut many of her declarative sentences, particularly those that begin "Turks are . . ." or "Muslims are . . ." or "Serbs are . . ." But much of this seems to be the product of being a female intellectual—questioning yourself would show weakness, and male peers pounce on female weakness. Your male peers understand feminine weakness better than feminine strength. And they know what to do with it.

But twenty-two-year-old women, fledgling intellectuals, need someone to look up to, someone they can recognize as kin and seek to emulate. The problem is when you hit twenty-eight and your role model's mediocrity begins to show, and you cringe in the way you cringed when you went to an Ani Di-

Franco concert for nostalgia's sake. God, did I ever really . . . But my twenty-two-year-old self appreciated the model, and I'm enjoying having West as my travel companion through (ex-)Yugoslavia even if sometimes I want to drown her in the bathtub.

* * *

The woman who looks after my apartment complex finds me sitting under her fig trees, reading Roberto Calasso and scribbling away. She speaks, I do not understand, and yet I nod and when she pauses I say *da da da*. I speak to her, of what I am reading and what I have seen in the city, and she does not understand, and yet she nods and when I pause she says *da da da*.

In the morning, I open my door and find she has left a pile of ripe green figs from the trees outside my window. They glow brightly, this little offering. I stand in my kitchen while the water for my tea boils, peel them open with my teeth, and feel their harsh fuzz against the roof of my mouth. It is the seeds I like, biting into them and breaking them, and even at 6 a.m. they are already radiating the heat they absorbed from the sun.

Perhaps she has noticed I have stopped leaving the apartment, except to buy more watermelon and more vodka. I feel safer here where there are women. I can hear my neighbor singing through the wall, but I never once catch a glimpse of her. If the caretaker left a trail of figs that led into town, I might make it past the iron gate. As it is, though, I get as far as the trees and I sit myself down.

* * *

From my station in Serbia and his station in California, my editor and I are trying to pull together a magazine devoted to Chicago. After business is taken care of, he asks, "So where are you right now?"

"Belgrade. I kind of hate it."

"One of my dearest friends lives in Belgrade now! You should e-mail him, see if he's in town." It is best never to question coincidences like this, one should always just run toward them with arms open wide. I e-mail Igor the second I end the Skype session, he writes back within minutes to schedule dinner.

There are no taxis, and so I take the bus. From the outer reaches of the city approaching the center, the place looks like a post-oil dystopia. The Brutalist concrete apartment buildings, thick tangles of wires going in through windows and doorways, clustering and disseminating. The off-the-grid tiny houses with roofs of tin, bottles and tubs filled with water lining each porch. Bombed-out buildings, done in by NATO, are left to slowly fall apart next to upright buildings where people go to work. And always, the dogs roaming free.

I get to the city center early, and so I circle the streets and alleyways of the pedestrian area. The city is vaguely familiar in that Central European way, all faded glamour and communist gloom side by side with postcommunist overexuberance mostly expressed in neon. Already, knowing I will have a companion, I am feeling a bit braver. The heat has finally relented somewhat, and the city's inhabitants come out to play. Everyone seems to be out tonight, parading back and forth, children running about and couples holding hands. I buy a bag of popcorn with the change in my pocket as smells of food hang thickly in the hot air and make my stomach rumble. Ears of corn, roasted nuts, sausages. They spark the appetite for the first time—I opened the refrigerator today only to stick my head into it to cool down. The crowd is intense, and there is music, loud, coming from somewhere. It has a polka beat but with a bass line overextending itself into fuzz and half of the musical instruments sounding synthetic. Groups of teenagers drape themselves around the fountains, the girls leaning forward and whispering, the guys leaning back and issuing loud commands. The sidewalk cafés are all full, with cigarettes being waved and liters of beer dropped loudly on tables.

I finish my popcorn and sit at our appointed meeting spot, under the statue of a man unknown to me sitting majestically on a horse, and wonder which of the men here will be Igor. I awkwardly try to make eye contact with a few men walking in my direction, but they look to the side hurriedly, coming near only to fetch a wayward child or greet someone else. One winks, and I drop my gaze quickly. But then there is the man who returns my questioning look with recognition and it is Igor, more handsome and younger than I had expected. He pulls me away from the square and into a whole other Belgrade.

We duck into what looks like a nondescript restaurant from the outside, but inside it is grand piano and velvet drapes and twinkling candlelight. The booths have heavy curtains that can be drawn, for all of your clandestine needs. We leave ours open but giggle when the overweight polyester man and the svelte young thing across from us close off their table. We order wine and lamb and more wine and coffee, and we are talking like old friends. Then I remember he is a potential "source," being native to the area, being a witness to the war—I should steer the conversation to that whole thing. I mention the episode of *Prime Suspect*, the one with the Bosnian victim. Igor stares at me without speaking for several seconds.

"That is absurd." That is the thing about this filter we—we being the people not of the Balkans—have chosen to discuss this war, this idea of "ancient hatreds." It makes the war inevitable. Therefore we, the international community, bear no responsibility for standing by and doing nothing: those crazy fuckers were going to go at each other no matter what, it was just a matter of time.

Igor stabs at his food. "There have not been reprisals. If this were about ancient hatreds and ethnic divisions, there would be revenge killings, there would still be fighting. This is a small country, everyone knows who did what." Igor is Bosnian; he and his family lived in Sarajevo during the siege, until escape was possible . . . But that is not my story to tell, even if it is a tremendous story. I am simply the outsider, the listener. I would get the references wrong, draw the wrong conclusions. I would write declarative sentences that start with "Serbs are" and "Muslims are." There is too much subtlety, there are too many ideas I carried into Belgrade, rather than coming to the city blank. I give West a hard time for being unable to shed her point of view as a British (a colonial, white, wealthy nation) citizen, and yet I know I have not shed my own either.

Even my question is naive, but I ask it anyway: "Did you ever think after all of that you'd be living in Serbia?"

"No. But then I fell in love with a woman who lives here, so I live here." He shrugs and grins.

Now we are on common ground again, a shared experience. Derailed by love. We leave the restaurant that moves like an opera house, and we relocate to a sidewalk café and drink a beer. He nods at the table next to ours, he knows one of the women, we are introduced. Also at the table is a journalist, American, here to write about Serbia. "Are you writing about the war?" He eyes me suspiciously.

"No." I try to soothe him with my harmlessness, my lack of competitiveness. "Rebecca West."

He nods, drinks from his bottle of beer, and turns his back. Igor and I pick up our thread of conversation, speaking of love lost and strange and acrimonious. I could drift here forever, but we are both responsible human beings with jobs and lovers and full inboxes, and so he hails me a cab and I glide home to get ready to depart the next morning for Sarajevo.

* * *

From the coach, riding into Sarajevo, my first thought is that it looks overwhelmingly familiar. I feel oriented, despite never having been here. And then I realize why: I saw all of these buildings on the television being shelled, or shot from, or housing nests of snipers. I saw people running for cover in the shadows of these buildings, and I saw the bodies of Sarajevo's "Romeo and Juliet," who were murdered on the bridge we just drove over. I remember the mountains and the trees that surround the city because I saw footage of men setting up artillery there. I saw newscasters filling us in on the latest statistics before the entertainment segment discussed Madonna's latest lifestyle choices.

My brain is a double negative, it is overlaying images in front of my eyes, the past and the present. Or maybe the city itself has done that with its unpatched bullet holes, the craters left from shells filled with a dark red resin, every mark made by the enemy worn as a proud scar.

I am renting a room from Tare, who is very nice and very good at ducking my awkward questions about the war. "How long have you lived in Sarajevo?" I ask him. "All my life." "Oh, so you were here during . . ." "For my whole life, yes." I imagine, given the dozens of eight-hundred-page books about the war by American and British authors that line the shelves of the bookstore here, that every single inhabitant of the city has been poked and prodded by journalists asking, "So that war thing. What was it like?"

Instead we talk about rock and roll, we talk about life in America. We talk about the cats that run around the city, all so clean and well fed for strays. "People didn't have enough food for them too, so they turned them out," thinking they would have more luck with the mice and the birds. They did okay for themselves. Now they are taken care of by everyone and are perfectly tame. At dusk I watch them walking down the street, crying at the window of a house until a bit of something is thrown out to them; then they go to the next house, like a nightly trick or treat. When they stop by my place I throw out bits of steak, the wings from my roasted chicken.

One morning I walk out of the bathroom wrapped in a towel, and a cat is on my couch, blinking at me. She leaves lazily via the open window, slinking between the iron bars that guard against entry. I laugh at her insolence, and at that moment a second cat darts between my legs and follows her friend back outside. Cheeky.

* * *

In all of the pages of *Black Lamb* there is something missing: Rebecca. Not Rebecca West the Historian, the Intellectual, the Analyst—they are all there. The Rebecca who shows up in the book is stiff and cold. When West writes about herself in the book, guiding us through a monastery or late-night café, interacting with her translator and guide Constantine or her husband, she becomes an intellectual viewpoint rather than a character. Her conversation spills out in perfectly structured paragraphs that succinctly summarize her point of view. She does only things that are thoughtful and measured. Nothing unexpected happens.

She omits Rebecca the human being. The woman who, while her husband slept in their Zagreb hotel room, was writing tortured letters to her lover back in England. Rebecca the not-so-great mother who would be taken apart in books by her son, accusing her of all sorts of crimes of neglect and indifference. The Rebecca who maybe cried when she was tired and overwhelmed, the Rebecca who hit the sauce, the Rebecca who played Candy Crush on her smartphone when she should have been meeting a deadline.

The problem of the son is an interesting one. The biographers sure like to spend time on it. Anthony was the product of Rebecca's affair with the married H. G. Wells, and it wasn't so much that he resented being a bastard as he resented having a mother who worked. I wonder when he noticed the difference, that his mother was not the perfect English housewife but was instead a writer of great ambition. I wonder when he started to feel entitled to a mother of the first variety. I wonder if Rebecca ever thought back to her childhood, with her good-for-nothing father, the poverty that made them retreat from London back to Scotland, the neglect and the added responsibilities of being a member of a not-quite-holding-it-together family. Surely that is one of the feeder streams of the ambition that eclipsed her excellence, if we want to be reductive. The sense of impending lack. The knowledge of what can happen when you lose your grip for one moment. I wonder if she saw what she persevered through and the hardship that had made her stronger, and thought every time she turned to her manuscript instead of her son, *He'll manage*. Instead of managing, he hoarded every slight and every maternal misstep and flung them back out into the world in the form of his "novel," *Heritage*. And in case people missed the similarities, he pointed out how much the characters resemble his parents and himself.

West's biographers and critics still judge her, and their tone goes harsh when they mention the poor hurts of the neglected son, not noticing they have perhaps in their heads cast their own mothers in the role of Rebecca West. It proves I am not the only one who still has some issues with an ambitious woman. (My problems with certain ambitious women are never how it affects their sons, it's how they tend to take on the characteristics of men in order to compete with them. It is so often the more terrible characteristics, the chauvinism, the unswayable certainty, the counting of success in dollars. West picked up the colonial mindset and an undying need for importance.) We all carry around our inability to forgive our mothers for whatever lack of attention or love that we think we suffered. And then we project our mother's face onto anyone who made similar choices, and we delight in being able to get our resentments out. Our fathers get free passes—our standards so low, he could miss a thousand ballet recitals, forget a dozen birthdays, misspell our name on our Christmas card (ahem, Dad) and we would still adore our fathers. Our mothers fail to read our mind and anticipate our needs and we are in therapy for years trying to get over that shit. Because Mr. West, while publicly condemning his mother, adored his rarely there and economically negligent father. But then we expect our fathers to lead by example, going forth into the world to show us how to exist out there ourselves. A little distance is to be expected and may be necessary. Our mothers, we're trained to believe, follow behind to catch us when we fall, or stay by our side to offer the consoling shoulder. If she's two steps ahead, then she is surely just leaving us behind, that selfish bitch.

Maybe that is why Rebecca does not show up in her own book except as a marble statue of Minerva. Intellectuals should be disembodied brains, and if not that then at least perfect representations of their philosophies. I once read an article stating that Simone de Beauvoir's submissive love for Jean-Paul Sartre made her great work *The Second Sex* entirely invalid. For years Mary Wollstonecraft has been derided by feminists and misogynists alike for her overwrought love life, which led her to fling herself into the Thames once or twice. That is what we think of intellectuals with messy lives. These little asides that critics make, they can stick in the brain like a knife. Rebecca's decision about her portrayal of herself can be seen as a form of protection.

But then how does a person be a person in Sarajevo? Am I allowed, in a city so often referred to as "war torn" and "besieged," to huddle in a doorway while trucks zoom past, crying on the phone with my lover? Am I allowed to be bored with the same trust-funded white boys playing at poverty who clutter every hostel in Central Europe? Am I allowed to admire the Muslim women's beautiful headscarves and covet one for my own? Am I allowed to be a shallow wreck, looking for rosemary oil with which to anoint myself to ease my heartache? Here, in a place where everyone has suffered so much more than I?

It's possible the city would prefer we didn't freeze its denizens in the moment of their greatest misery. Maybe they would like us to see them for something other than how well they suffered. Certainly the nation has contemporary problems that it needs to deal with, but it's only their acts that resemble war or violence that make news outside of this region.

Bosnia is suffering through a 40 percent unemployment rate, but the Western newspapers have decided that the Spanish best illustrate the economic crisis. The Spanish are more recognizable to us, they kind of look like us and live like us, we're familiar with them. Their suffering, then, we are better able to relate to.

Bosnia's youth are rioting in response to an ineffective, corrupt government, but we prefer Greece as an example of that. Greece is easier to understand, it's a presence in our cultural imagination. Plus its riots are more dynamic and its former government almost cartoonishly corrupt. We can't talk about Bosnia's government without talking about how the United States was instrumental in setting it up during the peace negotiations, and how we didn't seem to notice or care that we were bringing into power an arrangement that would obviously never work. Plus Greece, Bosnia, it's all kind of the same, yes? One should be able to stand in for the other.

The contemporary problems of Bosnia could never compare to its totally-sexy-in-an-action-movie-way tumultuous past. We did that, turned the suffering of the entire region into an action film starring big Hollywood actors. Owen Wilson ran in slow motion through a heavily mined landscape, Gene Hackman barked military orders, angelic choruses sang from on high. The American saved them all, of course. I don't think they hired even a single Balkan actor.

* * *

Igor e-mails, he tells me a friend is coming to Sarajevo and is staying only one block away from my sublet. We should have dinner. I embrace my coincidence. We meet in the old market, not at the restaurant that has the picture of the owner with arms wrapped around a boozy-looking Bill Clinton, at the one next to that. I am always early. I do not know how long I think it will take me to walk down one hill and then cross the street and around the corner and then there we are—I guess I thought it would take twenty minutes longer than it did.

I wear the long dress, the one we had to quickly purchase in Rome to gain entrance to the cathedral, the one that covers my scandalously female knees and shoulders. The sun has not quite gone down yet, and so the Ramadan streets are still. That is the secret to getting a good table, I was told—go when the population is fasting. The market is readying for the breaking of the fast, the smell of grilled meat and hot onions hitting you as you turn down the tiny-stone-paved alleyway.

The Leo sun is still roaring, and so I decide to wait at the table in the cool, dark depths of the restaurant. I order a plum brandy to keep me and Rebecca West company. Despite its stony weight, I packed her book in my purse. And then there is Peter, tall and handsome in an elongated, nerdy kind of way. Like a movie star playing a librarian, but stretched. I have a crush. He orders sour cherry brandy, but it is too sweet and too pretty to drink. It sits on the table between us untouched as we talk.

He, like me, is an outsider, a European, an explainer, here to gather information and relay it to a foreign audience. He tells me the concept of his book, very clever and poetic, an account of the former Yugoslavia told through the love lives of its inhabitants. He is interviewing Slovenian lesbians, Bosnian singles bars owners, Serbian divorcées. Even his title is very clever and poetic: *EX*. 'You are writing a better book than I am," I tell him. He smiles. "Well, you'll never know, because I am writing it in Dutch."

I have the urge to drink myself into liquidity and then pour myself into his pocket, and so I order more plum brandy. This will be our place, I decide, and that will prove to be true. Grilled meats, smothered in wild mushroom sauce, chased down with chilled brandy: these will be our evenings. We lay certain bits of information down on the table, the existence of his girlfriend, the name of my lover, and then don't pick them up again.

We walk back up the hill, back to our rooms. Separate rooms. We linger, not willing quite yet to dispel the ether between us, and then a stray cat's yowl distracts us and it is gone in an instant. I walk the rest of the way up alone. Somehow it's already the final call to prayer, I turn my head and a meteorite draws my attention upward. The unlit alleyway is not terrifying; somehow it is calming. The night clings close. I sit on the dusty rocks a few yards from where a destruction of feral cats is congregating. I had forgotten, tonight is the peak meteor shower.

The call to prayer continues, singing in many voices, coming from many directions. And one streak of light becomes two, becomes three. As a child dragged out of bed at 2 a.m. by my Carl Sagan–worshiping father, I would pick a section of sky and watch it closely, waiting for the meteors to move through it.

Waiting for the meteors to come to me. I would frustrate myself, angry when my sisters gasped and squealed as they saw stars fall while my chosen sky remained static. One has to open oneself up, take in the whole canvas without choosing, without discriminating. Relinquish focus and choose expansion. That is the song of the call to prayer. It moves you upward and outward, works you out of three dimensions and into four. Widen your scope, it sings. Unfix yourself. Allow yourself to move endlessly. Why choose a fragment when you can have the whole night sky?

My periphery opens. I lie back. The city sings, the cats purr, and the sky shifts and shakes.

*　*　*

I roll my eyes at Rebecca West. She is explaining. She is certain all Turkish men are one way. She is like the friend I respect and occasionally meet for drinks, only to remember why it's been six months since we last met the second she opens her mouth and starts telling everyone how great she is.

And yet there are moments I look up and realize how singular *Black Lamb* is. I'm still trying to understand what happened here, and so I watch a six-hour BBC documentary about the breakup of the nation and the march to war. But it makes it all seem so inevitable, and I am tired of hearing the phrase *ethnic tensions*. I flip through a well-respected Balkan expert's book; he is from England and he explains that only a totalitarian dictator like Tito could have kept a diverse nation like Yugoslavia together. These people, they need a firm hand to keep them from killing each other.

I read the diary of a man who survived the siege of Sarajevo, I watch a documentary about the beauty pageant held during the siege, all of the girls dressed up in heels and holding up a banner that says "Don't Let Them Kill Us." I read European justifications for not getting involved, I read conspiracy theories about the American bombing of the Chinese embassy in Belgrade.

And I realize the remarkable difference between all of those other books and Rebecca West's: West has women in her book. Other than the *Miss Sarajevo* documentary, the only women who appear in the other materials are shown weeping, openmouthed grieving, a wailing personification of aftermath. They don't speak except in cries, they don't have names.

But there are women in *Black Lamb and Grey Falcon*. They have names, they have ideas and lives and desires. Near the end of the book, as Rebecca and her companions work their way through Montenegro, they come upon a woman walking. Instead of passing her by or using her physical state to make pronouncements about the health of the region, about the poverty or oppression suffered, or using the way she dresses to allow her to stand in for an entire ethnic group, West talks to her.

Her first husband died, she tells West through her translator. Taken by the Austrians from their home and executed. Her two children also died. And it is not safe here to be an unmarried woman. So she married again and had two more children. Those children also died. Her second husband has now become senile and abusive. That is her life.

West and Constantine ask her if there is something they can do. They have a car—can they drive her to where she is going?

"I am not going anywhere," the woman tells her. "I am walking about to try to understand why all this has happened."

Critic Mary Mann calls this woman the "hero" of *Black Lamb*, and I agree with her. Because after the pageantry, after we lose interest in the Balkans again because of some other disaster somewhere else, some other conflict we can use for our metaphors, people will just be living their lives and getting on with it whether we are watching or not. Getting on with it is an act of heroism too.

* * *

Sarajevo has replaced the original plaque that marked the spot of Franz Ferdinand's assassination. According to West, it originally read, "Here, in this historical place, Gavrilo Princip was the initiator of liberty," but now it is blander and more direct: here is where one guy killed another guy. Perhaps after the siege the murderous acts of Serbian nationals were seen as less heroic.

The Sarajevo Museum picks up where the old plaque left off. It's a small room dedicated entirely to the assassination of Franz Ferdinand. And the first display case makes it clear it was very tragic, the murder of this man and his wife. Then, it suggests, as it tells you how it was the second assassination attempt of the day (someone threw a bomb into their carriage that morning), and how the whole thing was preventable and happened only due to incompetence and a long series of coincidences, maybe God just wanted him dead. The rest of the museum tells you all the ways in which this guy and the whole Austro-Hungarian Empire were a bunch of dicks who deserved far worse than they got. Then they have Princip's gun, and suddenly the museum is over and you step back outside into the heat and the noise of the market of modern Sarajevo.

And I love modern Sarajevo. The skyline of mountain and woods, the way the bats swirl above your head as you walk along the river at night. The weird sweet rosewater drink at the café. The exuberant friendliness of the people, the weekend evenings spent eating cevapi and drinking brandy while watching the parade of people walk by. I go and listen to Stravinsky and Schubert at the chamber music festival, held at a bullet-riddled opera house. Every morning I walk to the food hall and produce market, where the men lean over piles of tomatoes and eggplants and strange glowing purple beans I have never seen before to beckon me to this particular table, these particular eggplants. They flirt shamelessly, I shamelessly love it. But then I remember why this market looks familiar, it is the place where all of those people died. I remember the photos of the blood and bodies.

I go to see the first English-language movie I've seen in months, and in a city that was once under siege, I watch a movie based on a comic book about a city that is under siege. In the movie version, people cut off from the outside world apparently still have running water and supplies of shampoo coming in from somewhere, because their hair looks terrific. Electricity seems to be humming, gasoline supplies are making it in. I didn't know that is what the film was about, I just thought, *Oh there will be a car chase and things will blow up and I won't have to think for two hours.* But now I'm thinking too much, about how we present war as entertainment and suffering as metaphor. And I can't find an answer about how to bridge the terror of the past with the equally important needs of forgetting and remembrance. For walking around conscious and aware but without slipping too far into either cynical indifference or humorless stridency.

While I sit in Sarajevo we are in a season of revolution, just like 1989, just like 1968. North Africa is on the streets and Iran is getting bloody. After I leave here, Central Europe will join in the fight for something else, as will South America. And people will click on slideshows of the most apocalyptic views of the riots, and commentators will go on the air explaining how this is in their nature, this is a repeat of what these people did in this other year, the bloodiest day of fighting since comfortable year far in the past, and white Americans can feel secure that they will never have to face police officers cracking their heads, not unless they *seek it out*, that nothing, not even counts of how many protesters died in clashes with the police, with the army, will interrupt their primetime television schedule.

As I stand here in the city I do not know that Sarajevo will soon be the site of fiery revolt, that the archives that survived two world wars and the siege will burn as frustration with stagnation grows. Later these buildings first seen in pictures, then seen in person—they'll show up in the news again briefly, before Kiev is voted most interesting. I just walk home in the setting sun. Peter's leaving, I'm leaving, and we'll take our thoughts and our conclusions and our metaphors and we'll go back to our lives, where thinking about how to live with aftermath is theoretical or merely personal. I had longed for some sort of epiphany that would tell me how to live on blood-soaked ground and how to reckon with the past, and then maybe I could turn it into some sort of metaphor about my own life, connecting the war with particularly nasty things in the years prior. That would be too easy. The best we can do is keep walking, like the woman in West's story, trying to understand why all of this happened, but know, when we think we've found the answer, that our brains are only fooling.

South of France /
Margaret Anderson

> One has to be very sure of oneself to go against the ordinary
> view of things, and if one isn't, perhaps it's better not to run
> any risks, but just to walk along the same secure old road as the
> common herd. It's not exhilarating, it's not brave, and it's rather
> dull; but it's eminently safe.
>
> W. SOMERSET MAUGHAM

As I was packing for the south of France, my lover scanned a
map looking for my future location.

"Where is it again?"

I pointed: down near Cannes, near Antibes, flying into Nice.
"Everyone was there, or nearby. Maugham, Margaret, Picasso.
Graham Greene used to take his married lover down there."

"Also Hannibal. You'll be right where Hannibal came through
on his way to Rome."

"With his elephants?"

"Yes." He traced the route for me, up through Spain into
France, along the coast, then up and over the Alps.

"Tell me about Hannibal," I asked him, and he did. He re-
layed the history of the brilliant general, from his beginnings on
the frontier of a ferocious empire to his sudden death and the
destruction of his city. He told me that when he can't sleep at
night, he replays the Punic Wars in his head, moving Hannibal's
elephants over the mountains like sheep over a fence.

The alignment between the editor and the general made

sense, at least to me, the odd Midwestern girl and the invading army of ragtag rebels, mercenaries, and war elephants. Her route was no less radical than his. The odds were no less great. Hannibal was a brilliant military mind emerging from the fringes to nearly take down Rome. Margaret Anderson was a small-town girl who managed to center herself at the heart of modernism. The only discernible difference lies in the number of elephants employed.

* * *

Small-town girls from the middle of nowhere with no remarkable education or skill set simply do not do what Margaret Anderson did, which was assist in bringing about a revolution of the written word. In the early years of the twentieth century, she, armed with almost no formal education or ties to the art world, started a literary magazine whose influence is still being felt today. She named the mighty thing *The Little Review*, and with only her taste to guide her, she went about publishing the most exciting writing from the dawn of modernism. She helped to usher out that dreadful Victorianism that had lingered into the twentieth century, all Kipling and proper novels about proper subjects, to allow space for experimentation and radicalism. Everyone we still read and study from that era was published by her. While she produced no important writing of her own, she edited and published some of the most important work of the century, and she introduced writers to one another, and writers to their new audiences. She hung the transatlantic wires that allowed electricity to flow between worlds, allowed French literature to influence American, British to influence Russian.

And I like these people who jump extraordinarily between their birth and death data. Born a nobody in nowheresville. Died a madam of literature in the south of France.

The life of Margaret Anderson has a lot to teach a person about the power of the margins. Most of the writers she championed were the nerds and the fuck-ups, and of the writers she published and worked hard to promote, only a small smattering did not become canon. There was the psycho Ezra Pound, the mystic nerdboy W. B. Yeats, the pervy James Joyce, the sapphic Djuna Barnes, the farm boy Hart Crane, the radical weirdo Elsa von Freytag-Loringhoven. There was the aristocratic clique of Virginia Woolf and her vicious circle over in London, yes, plotting their own literary revolution. But Margaret picked up the more unlikely odds and ends, the writers who came from random places without connections or money or husbands with connections or money, and she gave them a stage. Because if you want to change the world, or even just a world, there are two ways to go about it. Either you can worm your way in, enfolding yourself into the mainstream and its methods and rhythms and social calendars and spread your disease and decay from there. Or you can lay siege from the outside.

To be fair, Margaret did not really have the opportunity for the first option. Growing up middle class or lower in a small town in one of those flyover states puts you at a powerful disadvantage with literary society. Without the opportunity to socialize with the children of the powerful, without a shared history, no old acquaintances from the Ivy League schools, how does one gain entry to *those* circles? Those circles that will get you jobs, introduce you to the people with money, put you in touch with agents and publishers and galleries and magazines and salons. It's not only for the sake of a job or a publishing deal, it's the life that you want. A life of the mind, as they call it.

But you're coming in from the fringes, from a Midwestern life of livestock and wheat fields and salads made of frozen peas, mayonnaise, and cheese cubes. "Here it is the Real," Margaret Anderson's lover and coeditor Jane Heap wrote about her

Topeka, Kansas, home. In the city, "it is Love and Art and Play." It is conversation and beautiful hats and opera boxes and champagne. It is being charming and witty and the throwing back of one's head to laugh when someone makes a joke, and it is the instant getting of that joke. (Never mind that this is not what life in the city is really like. In the fantasies of dirt road sophisticates, the urban lifestyle that plays in their heads looks like a nonstop bubble bath.)

It's not just that you were never taught the secret handshake that would gain you entry into a lifetime of Love and Art and Play. It's not just that your art education was necessarily self-acquired, the high plains not really being the place to find cutting-edge literature or see the exhibitions of the latest in sculpture, and it's not just that you, unlike everyone else at the party, when you finally do find your way to the party, pronounce all the names wrong and sometimes prefer, out loud, all the wrong people and paintings and had no idea there was such a thing as the wrong painting until you mentioned one in front of a bunch of people who all have on perfect eyeliner, even doing that little swoopy thing in the corner without even the slightest smudge because their hands apparently never tremble, and they all certainly know the secret handshake, and then one of them snorts and puts a hand on your arm and says, "Darling, no." It's not just that you eat and never learned to dine, that all of your clothing seems fashionable to you but to everyone else it screams Indiana department store. It's that they feel sorry for you.

Margaret Anderson did not give a fuck about option number one. Everyone who chooses to "make changes from the inside" risks simply getting absorbed and disappearing into the mass. They risk liking the feeling of acceptance and forgetting what their mission was in the first place. A person of a lesser character could waste decades of their life reshaping their mistaken opinions, refining their social graces, smoothing their rough edges through years of observation and mimicry. She, instead, decided it was all of them who were deluded, that having had the same education and the same families and the same socioeconomic backgrounds had resulted in groupthink, that this need to have the right opinion made society boring and conservative and wrong. Because she had had to shape her own education and personal taste through years of labor and scarcity, she had created original thought. She was free from the tyranny of being acceptable.

She was gifted with the same compensation that comes to anyone who is rejected by all comers: arrogance. And she honed it to a fine edge.

And so in 1914 Margaret started *The Little Review* in Chicago, and everyone she loved was invited to participate. She funded the thing through subscribers, who were pushed personally into it by Margaret, and little acts of random luck, like a friend's donation of a no longer necessary engagement ring. It started off as a magazine of criticism, but soon she saw that the position of critic was dependent on the publishing world and the publishing world was perhaps conservative and moribund. Critics are constantly reacting to other people's decisions rather than bringing beauty into the world themselves. She quickly realized she would have to start publishing the writing that she wanted to read, if she was going to read anything at all.

But first, before any of this, she would have to get out of Indiana.

* * *

Life is a glorious performance: quite apart from its setting, in spite of the kind of "part" one gets, everybody is given at least his chance to act. We may do our simple best with the roles we receive; we may change our "lines" if we're inventive enough to think of something better; we may alter our "business" to get our personalities across more effectively; or we may boldly accost the stage manager, hand back the part he'd cast us for, and prove our right to be starred.

MARGARET ANDERSON, introducing the first issue of *Little Review*

Margaret Anderson was suburban Indiana's nineteenth-century anomaly, the rest of it being pretty much golf clubs and bridge nights. From her own reports—and one only needs to read a few sentences of her memoirs to know she is a tremendous liar, so who knows what really happened—her childhood was one of deprivation. Not deprivation in a material sense but a deprivation of beauty. Which might not sound like much, unless you live on beauty, unless it is your air and water and religion. Despite the light touch she gives to her slim accounts of her home life, a shrug and a little laugh, you can feel weight behind the words: an anger that cannot be dismissed, a pressing down, as if you could still see traces of the manuscript where her beautiful penmanship is betrayed by marks from the snapping of the tip of her pencil, by tearing of the paper. These moments are mostly in regard to her mother.

Now, for a moment, I must interrupt myself to say a little something about us changelings. Because it is necessary to distinguish between the changeling and the black sheep. The black sheep, who would shudder to hear this and probably stomp off to his room to chip his black nail polish and make sure his parents can smell the pot smoke curling under his bedroom door, is a manufactured anomaly. His rebellion is staged and his identity shaped entirely by family interactions. That those interactions primarily consist in clashings and bangings does not change the fact that who he is is tied to his family. He tests the reactions and interactions—if I do this do you scream and yell, if I do that do you chase me out of the house and threaten to cut me off. Fine. Noted. He cultivates family members' discomfort and attempts to embody it.

Then there is the changeling, who came to this planet as an already fully formed creature, and whose identity has nothing to do with the people who raised her. The family's only influence is circumstantial; they cannot mold their little beast into something they can recognize as being of them. They can try. They do, often, brutally. But it is of no use, they are forever estranged, and whatever familial appearance she inherited—her father's nose, her mother's ash-blond hair—she will forever be identifiable as Other. It is as if as an infant she was swapped out for a fairy.

While the black sheep is still associated with the family, even if only in their grief and prayers, the mother wringing her hands and insisting he's a good kid, really, he just fell in with the wrong crowd, there is a rejection, almost bodily, almost immediately, that happens between the changeling and her family. The father may grow to be enamored with their beast as she grows up and begins to reveal who she truly is, all of her charms and glamours finally finding form, but the mother knows this one is not her own. And this . . . thing is taking her resources, disrupting the nest, and competing with her for the attention of her husband. As it was for Margaret, who spoke lovingly of her father, but not even her brandy-and-caramels writing style can hide her fury with the woman who rejected her. Under the gloss, one can see Margaret thinks of her mother as a heartless child-devouring lamia.

Perhaps we could find sympathy for the lamia that Margaret could not. It is not like motherhood was necessarily a choice in that time and place, even after technological breakthroughs. If the Midwest believes in utility above all, and it does, the utility of the female reproductive system is included here. And who knows what her mother would rather be doing with her time and with her body? Women who are shoved into motherhood aren't always able to raise themselves up to the soft-focus Hallmark visions of what it should be. And then on top of that to discover your womb was cuckooed, and the being that you sheltered and gave yourself to in the parasitic exchange is unrecognizable to you—it must be a shock. Disgust is a difficult emotion both to overcome and to disguise.

Being a changeling child is torment, as the child never quite understands why acceptance is being withheld, but for an adult, being beholden to no one is a thrilling little terror. Better than an orphan, even. Less paperwork. And we know from all of children's literature that orphans go on the biggest adventures. But that explains Margaret, the openly gay, Aphrodite and Apollo–worshiping aesthete, mistakenly delivered to the American Midwest.

* * *

When you are eight years old and in Kansas history class and they are trying to make you feel okay about coming out of a much-maligned region of America, because we all know that the coasts are where the important, intelligent people come from, they tell you about Amelia Earhart (but not the whole open marriage thing) and William Allen White (but not his progressive politics) and John Brown. They tell you all about John Brown, even his murdering of children, in a proud tone of voice because seriously, fuck those fuckers over in Missouri.

They don't tell you about the radicals like William Burroughs or Louise Brooks or anyone who left Kansas for a place that better suited them. They don't tell you there are other ways to live your life than church, community, family. They do tell you that the outside world is not so great, it is violent and lonely and disappointing. They tell you that unmet desire is the most unbearable thing in the world, and that no one ever recovers from not getting what they want. They tell you it is better not to want anything at all, you should be happy to have the little that you have, a plot of land, a series of obligations, a community that doesn't so much protect as police you.

I head up to Paris to meet with a fellow Kansan. We buy wine at the market and walk around the streets drinking from the bottle. When we run out, we sit at a café to order a carafe and to smoke. Me cigarettes, him a cigar. We fumble through terrible French with the waiter and watch silently as Paris walks by our table.

He raises an eyebrow. "Did you ever think?"

Not in my most fantastical moments lying in my childhood bed, wishing for variations on my future, did Paris ever come into it. My big dream was to become a high school English teacher. If I was lucky, maybe somewhere outside of Kansas, but let's not get crazy.

"No. Did you?"

"No. But that's the good thing about growing up in Kansas."

"Yes. Low expectations."

* * *

I don't know what I would have made of Margaret or her Topeka-born co-editor/lover Jane Heap had I been introduced to them way back then. If I had actually thought a life of the mind were a possibility for a changeling and a college dropout from a town of twelve hundred people, the weight of establishing it as a real goal and measuring how long it would take and how much work it required, might have crushed me before I started. Best, then, to stumble into it accidentally again and again and again.

Thinking something is impossible is actually a really good way to go about accomplishing it. When one feels that failure is inevitable, it frees one up for experimentation. It's that rigid *this must work* that narrows a person's perspective. Because look, we're not going to win the race to the summit, because we didn't wear the right shoes, and those people over there, they've been training all of their lives for this moment. And that's disappointing. But maybe if we just see how far we can get, maybe look for a different way around instead of storming directly up, we'll see some interesting things along the way. And a lot of times you were right, the summit is unattainable, but the attempt was much less desperate and much more fun than you feared. Beautiful things can happen in the act of failing.

But then I'm a Cancer. I've always been most comfortable approaching things from the side.

* * *

The Midwest was not kind to Margaret, but then it is kind to few. The Midwest god is a Calvinist god. A god of fear and tyranny, a god who displays his powers through brute force, whether that be tornado or epic drought. The Midwesterner is exposed, vulnerable below his fearsome thunder god and dependent upon his mercy. And haunting the Midwesterner is the belief that with just a little more work, a little more grit and determination, a little more groveling and self-annihilation, he can change his fate. And if his god responds unfavorably, the Midwesterner looks to find fault within himself, not the heavens.

The Midwest can tolerate a lot of eccentricity. It has to—it manufactures it the way it manufactures feed crops and aluminum siding. There is only so much standing people can do under the unblinking eye of an angry god before they find themselves in the garage turning the old tractor into scrap to build an eight-foot-high monster with the parts. That is something the Midwest understands, the way loneliness, living perpetually poised at the brink of financial devastation, and Reality slowly take a person apart.

What it doesn't tolerate is insubordination.

I have lost track of whether I am writing about Margaret Anderson or about myself. Our bios intermingle, her mother becomes my mother, my Chicago becomes her Chicago. When I look up a fact or a date in her memoirs, I pick up her writing style immediately, and when I notice it is her hand guiding my pen I have to tear out whole pages. But that too is part of coming out of a childhood of such an acute displacement: you dream so feverishly and so long of being someone else, somewhere else, placing yourself in a million different bodies in a million different places, anywhere but here, that it is not always so easy to come back to yourself.

* * *

We should be talking about Margaret in France, but I am reluctant to place her there. In France she found her spiritual home. How boring. Wouldn't we all just rather picture Hannibal moving elephants over mountains than winning battles against the Romans? And I am reluctant to go to France myself. I imagine my body in France eating seafood and drinking wine and feeling the sun on my skin and reading novels, and I feel nothing but dread. When I hear my flight is canceled because of a weather event and cannot be rescheduled for three days I am elated. France will just be picturesque and beautiful and the sea will crash against the shore and what is the point of any of it. Give me an unmovable obstacle and I am content. It is what I was trained for.

* * *

It is Margaret's hard climb out of her hometown that I am interested in. ("Hometown" conjures up images of a place of safety and comfort, a place of kissed bruises and hot chocolate on cold nights. "Place of birth" is probably more appropriate.) Columbus, Indiana, is not far geographically from Chicago, but it is another world. It seems obsessed with society in the way that only places utterly lacking in real society can possibly be. People wear their association with country clubs, family lines, church congregations, the Rotary Club versus the Lion's Club. It is not rural, it is suburban, in that closed-off, someone-complains-if-your-lawn-is-not-regularly-trimmed way. It is a safe middle, the physical embodiment of a too-strong dose of antidepressants. The lows cannot get too low, but then the highs elude you as well. (With probably the added sexual dysfunction side effect.)

But then the glamour of Chicago can be patchy, particularly when it comes to the arts. Chicago is built from its Midwestern people, and while most everyone got there via a full-tilt run, it is more difficult to shed that Calvinist indoctrination than one first expects. Your self-worth is still tied deeply to your productivity, that Protestant work ethic that will stay with you until your deathbed. Your loved ones will be surrounding you, the angels will be calling, and still you'll be adding up the value of your accomplishments in dollars and cents.

And what is the value of art? And don't give me any of your abstractions or "in a child's smile" bullshit. Muses have become the brands that might pay us to sell their products. Writers are expected not only to produce their work but to sell it. Their personality, their life story, all of it comes up on the market. The heart of Chicago beats in the Mercantile Exchange. Margaret Anderson started *Little Review* in Chicago, but soon she was needing to give up her offices, and then her home, and then she moved into a tent on the shore of Lake Michigan, because she could not convince the people of Chicago to invest in the future of writing and the future of art.

But the easiest thing is to go into nostalgia and pine for a day when art was pure and unsullied by the concept of the market. Let's be clear: even the Romans stashed their mint in the temple of the goddess Juno. Ever since there was money, it has been contaminating the divine.

(It is, however, equally easy to believe that we have been on some sort of upward progression, that everything in the past turned out to be a series of errors and corrections. The rational economic lens through which we have decided to examine everything, even art and love and sex and the soul and divinity, is the right one—everything else was trying to focus through astigmatism. It is difficult in a culture that believes in progress to convince people there were things that were discarded along the way that we might want to go back and fetch.)

* * *

Despite my prayers for an unpronounceable volcano to disrupt European travel for a month, my flight is rescheduled, and I fly into Nice. Hung over, with unwashed hair, and with a suitcase that suicided somewhere over the Alps and presents itself on the conveyer belt with exploded innards.

The south of France of today is what happens to a place when all the artists, the queers, and the misfits have been driven out by rising prices and improving "quality of life." The rich are attracted to the places built by the freaks, the heat and the noise of places like Berlin, New York, San Francisco, and then they strip the cities down to their stumps like an insect swarm, driving off any biodiversity until all that is left is people with money.

And the freaks did flock here between the Wars, mostly Brits and Americans who left their cold, conservative homes to learn about art and culture. And many, like W. Somerset Maugham, like Margaret Anderson, were queer and able to breathe a little easier and more openly than in their homeland. The weather was beautiful, the cost of living was low (unstable governments and economies do have their upsides, after all), and here art was a value, not a commodity.

Most of these Americans and Brits returned to whence they came to live in the suburbs and do that whole arrangement, because when culture confronts capital, capital almost always wins. And as France stabilized and the people with money smelled fruitful fields just ready to be stripped down, the transformation began.

This little village's marina, where idealistic little paintings of fishing boats and the dappled sun coming off the water used to be painted, is now thick with slick, oily rainbows and clogged with absurd yachts. Facing it is the same blocky architecture with cookie-cutter condos that fortifies every shoreline now that a beautiful view has been commodified. The markets sell mostly rich people's picnic food—I can find eight different types of dark chocolate with hazelnuts, but no dried beans. The restaurants all serve fifteen-dollar house-created cocktails named after the artists who could never afford to drink them. I'm drinking something with gin named for Colette, and it's sweet where it should be acidic. It's being paid for by an old man in a yachtsman cap and an ascot who is using his limited English to explain to me how beautiful I am. I'm sure his wife is here somewhere, in the masses of women with Pilates-and-silicon-rehabbed bodies and eyes pulled alarmingly back and up. One of them looks at me, pointedly looks at my poor person's clothing and then back up at my face. *Oh, don't worry, bitch*, I think as I slurp another oyster. *I'm judging you, too.*

A little tipsy, I walk to Cannes, or at least I walk to the fence that surrounds the Cannes airport, and I watch the private jets fly in and out. The building roar of takeoff, the powering down of landing. It's as rhythmic and hypnotic as the sea.

* * *

There was one final thing that pushed Margaret out of the United States. She was living in New York City, holding salons and editing *The Little Review*, which had recently begun serializing James Joyce's *Ulysses*. *The Little Review* was at its peak, publishing once a month and presenting the best literature and art from the era. She was associating with the revolutionary Emma Goldman and living openly as the lover of her coeditor Jane Heap and another lover, Gladys Tilden.

One of these acts would get her into considerable trouble.

In 1921 Margaret Anderson and Jane Heap went on trial for obscenity charges relating to their serialization of *Ulysses*. Issues were confiscated and destroyed, and the magazine had been always teetering on the edge of financial ruin as it was. They had been unable to convince New York publishers to support them with ads, several of whom having given as the reason a desire to stay distant from controversial contributors like Joyce. (Margaret Anderson was told by a publisher "that they regard us as a literary curiosity and preserve back numbers of *The Little Review* as a record of the insanity of the age.") Their only financial support came through subscribers and donations that added up to a few hundred dollars a year.

The case made all the papers. Their subscribers and friends showed up in strong numbers for moral support, but as important as moral support is, it does different work from financial. Just as the support of peers does different work from institutional support. But surely now the publishing world would rally around them. This wasn't simply a case of one writer who is not to everyone's liking and is still the bane of college students the world over, judging by all of his Amazon one-star reviews. This was about how decency acts as a bully, about the fascistic heart of the prude.

And okay, maybe the section that Margaret and Jane chose to serialize was the Nausicaa chapter with the guy jerking off as he watches the girl waggle her legs, and maybe that did not help matters. And maybe they had established an antagonistic relationship with New York and Boston publishers, calling them cowards and faint-hearted prigs in their editorials. And maybe the fact that she wasn't politely discreet about those other things that she was doing, like being gay and talking about anarchy, made her tricky to publicly support. But that shouldn't matter, and the fact that it did revealed that she was right all along. The publishing world was made up of cowards and faint-hearted prigs.

Margaret Anderson and Jane Heap were brought to trial on obscenity charges, they were publicly declared to be a "danger to the minds of young girls," and Margaret cracked jokes about how they were never able to assemble a jury of her true peers anyway. "Where ever could they be found?" They were found guilty, they were fined, the magazine was destroyed, and they were left penniless.

Margaret Anderson and Jane Heap left for France.

* * *

(Once the danger had passed, and publishers started to realize that people were undertaking extreme measures to obtain copies of *Ulysses*—Joyce's publisher in France, Sylvia Beach, sent men with copies stuffed down their pants on the ferry from Canada to the United States over and over and over again and still could not meet the demand—and so therefore they could probably make some money off this, Random House challenged the ban, won, and over the years made a great deal of money from it. Almost all of the writers published in *Little Review* would become profitable, once the editors of the little modernist magazines helped to rub the sheen of scandal off their work.)

* * *

Being kept from what it is you desire can be like the long pull back of a slingshot. If you don't break the tension and slump down discouraged in the process, of course. All those years of being thwarted, ignored, neglected, and discouraged was just the drawing of the rock and the steadying of the aim. You fear that the relief will never come, that you will be split apart by the tension or your strength will fail. But then . . . release, and over the Atlantic she goes.

* * *

Hannibal wasn't as pro-Carthage as he was anti-Rome. He hadn't lived there since he was a child, dwelling instead on the Iberian frontier of the Phoenician Empire. And anyway, Carthage was not that great. The city was powerful, sure, but it seemed to have a bad tendency to throw its firstborn sons into a flaming incinerator. And crucify, in a cross-and-nails kind of way, not in an emotional, metaphorical kind of way, the people who disagreed with them. Or they didn't, maybe, but everyone thinks they did. That is what happens when your enemy burns all of your history books and writes your story for you.

And it's not that Carthage was so great as it is that Rome was not so great. Post-Punic, it turned out to be like every other corporate entity, more concerned with growth than with genius. Completely unconcerned about the way it fed itself with whatever was in its way. And if a problem arose, it had no better way to deal with it than to throw money and bodies at it until the problem went away, which is what it did with Hannibal. To battle a hulking madman, you can't meet force with force. You have to be willing to be ridiculous. (One of Hannibal's ideas was to throw jars filled with venomous snakes onto the enemy's ships during battle. The jars would break and the snakes would attack the sailors.) I think it's more difficult to allow yourself to be ridiculous when everyone around you is participating devotedly in the status quo. Off in the fringes, where you are having to make do with what you have, experimentation is the rule.

And by the way, Hannibal's name means "Sacred to the Mountain God." Of course he went over the Alps.

* * *

The thing that annoys me about Margaret's memoirs is that she is so lah-de-dah about all of it. About the ostracism, the financial ruin, the rejection and persecution and injustice. When she has to move out to a tent on the shore of Lake Michigan, she makes it sound like the world's most fabulous picnic. If she were run over by a bulldozer, her greatest complaint would be that it chipped her nail polish. It's all just one long *experience* for her. Three volumes of recollections and never once does she recall herself drunk and sobbing on the floor.

I am drunk and sobbing on the floor.

I mean, sometimes. I am so bored here in the south of France with no one to talk to, nothing to see or do. There are nightclubs, restaurants I can't afford, parties I am not invited to. I cannot seem to distract myself from myself, and it's not like I am such good company. If only there were an opera to lose myself in. Something enormous that opens up and swallows you, something to take you into the archetypal and out of the personal. I scan the events listings online; the only thing playing is a production of *Carmen* three cities over. I miss the old rich, when the elite took pride in cultural elitism and not just financial, even if their idea of good culture was a composer who died at least fifty years before. The new rich, from the nerdboys with their adolescent kingdoms to these playboys and heiresses, are so hopelessly suburban in their tastes. I guess I can walk down to the beach again and go climbing over their castle, but it kind of lost any allure it had once I learned it was built in the twentieth century. Probably the decision of some rich person, someone who thought they could just buy the history that they wanted.

So at 5 p.m. I pull down the bottle of wine and slowly empty it through the night, reading books about the Russian Revolution and feeling a drunken glee at the humiliations of the rich oppressors. Not that the poor oppressed turned out to be any great shakes. I can't imagine anything good would come from a cultural revolution born out of the Midwest, but for a moment I like the idea of my people taking revenge for every bestiality joke, every eye roll over blind religious faith, every stereotype of the dumb hick and small town naïf. It's satisfying, the image of a pitchfork in the middle of one particular editor, but then it would go badly quickly. Besides, I don't even remember ever seeing a Kansan with a pitchfork in real life, now that I think about it.

And it's not that I want to read about Margaret being weepy. I would rather picture her furious. I want her to throw a brick through Random House's window. I want Bennett Cerf to be mysteriously pulled to his backyard window, and I want him to be startled to see Margaret out there, under the lamplight, in her fur stole and pearls, cigarette dangling from her mouth, middle finger extended.

Drunk and climbing into bed, I decide on a different route. Over the Alps, not by sea. I'll start a literary magazine of my own. I'll call it *Spolia*, a Roman term, why not. It means to use rubble to build a new structure.

* * *

The Little Review did not last long once Margaret got to France. The issues dwindled in frequency immediately following the trial, and then they stopped altogether. Money was one problem. She'd never had much, but recovering from several issues being destroyed by the United States government was too much.

And then there had to be the question, unarticulated in the ever-optimistic memoirs, "who am I doing this for anyway?" It's not easy to maintain an abstract idea of your audience. You requires some sort of acknowledgment from the world before we all just resign ourselves to the misery that lies at the bottom of the whiskey bottle. Having the mechanism behind the work you live and die for reject you entirely is not easy to walk away from. You can say all you want, I am doing this for the sixteen-year-olds in Indianapolis who are starving for beauty, but without some sort of compensation, like fame or money or respect, there's only so much of your soul to pass around to others.

There's also the possibility that France met Margaret's needs. The area at the time was absolutely everything she had longed for. Writers and intellectuals and composers and philosophers and painters and poets and aesthetes, all packed together in one region and sharing wine and work and conversation.

Lack is one of the world's greatest motivators. The lack that not even financial success can fill. The need for something internal or external—that is what drives us back to the table, or the easel, or the theater hall again and again. It's very revealing, the moment a person finds satisfaction and can put the work aside. Is it when the big award is won? When the husband and baby have been found and secured? When the bank account is full? When there's a different seventeen-year-old taking off their pants for you every night? When do you stop growing or fighting or chasing? Or do you never stop, still struggling until your last moments to get at it. And which is a more depressing way to live?

It never seemed like the work was that important to Margaret; it was the *life* that she wanted. And once she had the life in place, once she didn't have to earn her way into it by publishing the people she wanted to surround herself with, the magazine served little purpose.

She was right to reject the established American literary society and make her home among the marginalized in France. What is required to achieve approval among the gatekeepers and the tastemakers and the publishers and the people of power would have diluted her, and we need Margaret Anderson as the strong brew.

She found a guru. She went to concerts. She wrote loopy little memoirs. She seduced a lot of straight women. Why bother with all the rest of it?

* * *

Hannibal was eventually defeated, after turning away from Rome too soon. Carthage was destroyed. The soil was sown with salt, the wells were poisoned, and their reputation was slandered by their victors. Bennett Cerf is now considered to be the publisher who brought *Ulysses* to America, and one of the most important figures in literature's great twentieth century. Margaret Anderson's memoirs are all out of print.

But then again, it was the life she was after, not the afterlife. All of the government's talk about how she was a danger to the minds of young girls, I say, yes. And thank god for that.

Galway / Maud Gonne

You lose things when you travel. I lose so much underwear that I've become convinced someone just follows me around Europe taking it out of my bag as I sleep. I leave a trail of discarded books and misplaced pens everywhere I go. And then it's always the small stuff, the sentimental stuff, that can fall under beds or behind dressers and you won't miss it until you're three countries over.

I don't remember when I noticed I was missing a necklace, but once I did I was pretty sure which hotel room I had left it in. I felt very attached to this necklace, although I didn't wear it much. A single pearl, cupped by a silver shell, tight around the throat. I had bought it in New York City, during the first trip there I had made on my own.

But I had been studying the Golden Dawn, and Maud Gonne, and I thought maybe a little magic would help when the lost and found at the hotel failed me. My mentor in the subject told me the fairies are always willing to help with these sorts of things, if you're nice to them. So I smeared some butter outside my window, left out a little shot glass of whiskey, and asked them to find my necklace. Then I forgot about it.

Hours later, I was on my way to bed. I opened up the bedroom door and a large moth flew directly at my face. I reached for the first thing I could find to swat at the thing, which was an old glove lying on the dresser. As I picked it up, my missing necklace slipped out of it and onto the floor.

I looked up, the moth was gone. And I screamed, and ran out of the room.

* * *

The first thing that should be said about Maud Gonne is that she is not Irish. You might be confused about this, seeing as how she lied all the way through her memoir about her connection to Ireland, and how she became a kind of living symbol of the nation as she campaigned to drum up rebellion against the English occupying force. But no, she was born to a captain in the British Army, and other than a brief stay in Ireland to heal her tubercular lungs with the good Irish air, she did not spend much time in the country until she was sixteen and her father was stationed (as part of the occupying force) in Dublin.

But then other things she left out of her memoir include her selling her soul to the Devil as a teenager, the ritual of resurrection she performed to reimpregnate herself with the soul of her dead son, and the fact that after she turned down William Butler Yeats for marriage for the eightieth or so time, he asked if he could marry her daughter instead and she said sure. (The daughter thought about it and said no thank you.)

There was an idea that Maud Gonne was very interested in projecting, and that was herself as an embodiment of the spirit of Ireland. And the spirit of Ireland could hardly be British. But her story, the real one, of a life as an actress turned revolutionary turned black magician turned allegory, is as complicated as the story of Ireland itself.

* * *

I sit in my Galway apartment, which smells of damp and all of the ways we try to combat damp, like central heating and closed windows. There is only a little bit of sun every day, and I try to put myself directly in its path, sitting right in front of my southern-facing glass doors. While I wait for the clouds to part and feeling to come back into my cold toes, I read about anxiety and its contrast to fear. According to Rollo May, the difference is in the force that opposes you. With fear you have an object, a power or a person or a circumstance that could harm or destroy you. As a result, your body readies itself for battle, for the physical act of conquest that must happen. You focus in on your opponent, and all else fades away.

With anxiety you are never sure what you are afraid of or from where the harm could come. You know there is something out there, shrouded in darkness, but god knows what it is. Does it have pointy teeth or perhaps a honed sword? Will it wait until your back is turned, or will it rush you from where you stand? Or will it spit its venom from afar and you'll die before knowing what it was exactly that took you down? Because the danger remains indefinable, the body achieves a constant, wide-open vigilance, always on the lookout for anything that poses a threat. And when you cannot name your fear, when you cannot identify the presence stalking you, all comers look like adversaries.

Perhaps the Central European states, ruled by fear, had an easier go of it. They knew who the enemy was—it was the state. And the way to keep the state at bay was to maintain a strict self-control, because it was clear what would happen if you stepped out of line. Torture, imprisonment, or maybe you would simply fall out of favor in a time when being in favor meant all.

And no wonder, then, that the states ruled by fear, once the enemy had been defeated—the Czech Republic, the DDR, Poland—recovered so quickly and transitioned so brightly.

The British did not rule Ireland with fear, they ruled through anxiety. First they destroyed the Irish language to bring about disorientation. Then they repeatedly changed the rules of acceptable behavior so that no one was ever immune from punishment. Then they used random acts of violence and tyranny to destabilize a sense of security. But their finest moment had to be the Irish Famine, a little weapon of war they lucked into. They were allowed to drive off a quarter of the population through death or displacement and then actually convince the Irish that this was their own fault: It's divine retribution, you see. And we cannot possibly help you, because all of that other food you are growing, all of those food animals you have raised and fished from the sea, that's just ours. And we cannot spare any of it, we really can't. Maybe if you had not been so wicked . . .

Yes, the British ruled the Irish through anxiety, forever obscuring the source of the next attack until most didn't even notice when the enemy withdrew. And so the Irish turned on themselves. Men against women, the Jesuits against the children in their care, Catholic against Protestant, the self against the self.

This is what Maud Gonne was born into in 1866, just a few years after the peak of the Famine. These are the sins of the father she set out to put right.

* * *

Her first step was to sell her soul to the Devil. And if her biography had been written out by E. T. A. Hoffmann, he would have set it up exactly the same way.

Maud was a girl rebelling against her British military father by making impassioned arguments for Home Rule and cavorting with the Resistance. One night as she was rummaging through her father's library, she came across a book about black magic. Reading it late into the night, she declared aloud that the Devil could have her soul if he gave her control over her own existence. At that moment the clock struck midnight, and she believed her request had been heard. Within a fortnight her father was dead, and she devoted herself to undoing what he had devoted his life to doing.

But we must go back to this idea of what she had sold her soul to the Devil *for*. Control of her own life. It wasn't just the ever-present fear in all nineteenth-century women with a brain that she would be shackled to some dull-witted inbred aristocrat and have the focus of the rest of her life be what went in and out from between her legs. And it wasn't just finding the money to be an independent woman so she could do some sort of Grand Tour of European hotels and society. The whole point of black magic is to work it so that your will can be done. It is the opposite of the Christian concept of Thy Will Be Done and We Will All Just Sit Around and Try to Adjust. That was the attitude of the Irish Catholics after they had been stripped of their educational system and language, stripped of any hope of prosperity, stripped of any evidence that there was such a thing as free will. That was what they clung to when they clung to their churches. Black magic was a way to say, I do not move for the universe, the universe moves for me.

Maybe we need a black magic revival now that our atheist philosophers and scientists have presented us with a materialist world. Somehow that is where the hardcore Calvinists and the atheists have chosen to intersect: at the dismissal of free will. For the materialists, though, it is not God running the show, it is our goddamn biology. We are slaves to our unconscious impulses, our evolutionary data, our autonomic system of hormones and endorphins and neurotransmitters. Your depression is just an imbalanced chemistry, and you may think that you chose to eat that salad, but your system—responding to the smell of bread wafting out of the bakery and your blood sugar levels and your advertising-addled brain that tells you this is the *best* salad because you are associating it with happiness and sexual prowess somehow—chose your salad for you. You are just a bag of meat, dimly aware of your own world.

And love is just an overdose of sexual hormones and endorphin levels and the way someone smells based on the compatibility of your conjoined immune systems to produce healthy offspring, and reproduction is just a biological instinct implanted in us to ensure the survival of the species, et cetera.

If given the choice between a materialist worldview and an irrational black magic practice, I choose black magic. My first act of free will is to choose to believe in free will.

* * *

If Maud is the embodiment of all of Ireland, then I figure I can land anywhere I want to here. I end up in Galway, where there is a free apartment and a kind of sort of acquaintance. I had lived in Cork for a while, years ago, and it is reassuringly near.

Nora Barnacle lived just up the street. I keep trying to visit her house, but there are no posted open hours, and no matter what day of the week or hour of the day I try to visit, no one opens up. It is the kind of house that is described as "charming" and "rustic" in the pages of real estate ads—a traditional Irish cottage!—all of these reclaimed houses no one can pay for anymore. In reality, though, it just looks cold and dark and sad.

Somehow I have slipped. I have to sleep with my computer right by the bed just in case I wake up and start having thoughts. My thoughts need constant interruption, as the stickiness of it will never work, things will never get better, all is lost, the sea wants to have a conversation with you—it all traps me in the same place. I have television, blogs, social media all queued up to keep me from having thoughts.

I have been studying Yeats's Golden Dawn notebooks, but it all seems so pointless. What would the end of that study be? To get what I want? I have forgotten how to want. Every few days I buy the same things at the grocery store: roast chicken, potatoes, brussels sprout. Nothing really has to taste like anything, and I don't have to figure out what I'm craving. If I asked myself that, I would sit down in front of the dairy case and weep, they would have to pull me out of there like a sad wet sack.

There are people starving in such and such places, but measuring-stick suffering never makes one feel any better.

"Maybe you should take up yoga, or meditation," says the Irishman to me.

"I hate yoga, all of that breathing. Plus, the people are terrible."

"Yes, the people are terrible. But it would perhaps help you get control of your thoughts."

I do my best: I walk past a yoga studio and head to the bookstore instead. My thoughts don't need control, only replacement, by people's better thoughts. Even at 2 a.m., a Robert Graves thought is a wonderful thing to have on hand.

* * *

I keep watching the footage from the Romanian 1989 revolution, over and over again, the moment when it turned. They were late, other governments throughout communist East and Central Europe had already fallen. The Ceauşescus kept a tighter grip, the fated quality of their reign discouraged any movements against it. And then there was a rally, small and containable, because things had been bad for so very long. The official response looked like it was going to be the same as always—let them blow off some steam, let them feel their voices had been heard, show strength and understanding, then disperse.

It went wrong. There were what sounded like shots fired and some screams. And Ceauşescu, he flinched. He showed fear and confusion. The TV news, whose sole job was to reinforce the government, shut off the live feed in fear of showing a weakened leader, so that the last thing the entire nation saw before the screen went blank was not a leader carved from stone, not an omnipotent god who could read their thoughts and send the Securitate to punish the bad ones, it was a confused old man. Their enemy showed vulnerability. And within minutes Bucharest was out on the streets, the protests swelled and they expanded into a riot. The people could not fight a god, but they could defeat an old man. The government fell.

(Only to fall into the hands of the secret police, who quickly executed the former leaders to distract the public from who was taking over hidden under the cloak of justice, and it would take a while before people realized what was going on. None of that changes the remarkable act of a people who set aside their fear.)

* * *

The river outside my apartment window moves like a motherfucker. It is as black as ink and swift. It has places to be, and it pulls under all who fall in. As you walk along the quay, there are life preservers every few meters, but looking at this little ring and back at this river, you know those drops of water you just saw whiten at the crest as it flings and is flung, those drops have gone out to sea in the time it took you to turn your head. A body, once you've undone the latch, once you have taken aim, it would be down deep. How deep? I'll let you know when I get down there.

The river, it hypnotizes. It murmurs and it calls. Also as evenly spaced out as the life preservers are suicide hotline numbers on little placards.

It is gray here. The sea, the sky, the stone buildings. The black river is the only variation. No wonder so many take a dive. I picture it myself every time I walk alongside it, feeling its relent-less pull. "Not today," I tell it.

* * *

"It's learned helplessness," the historian Tim Pat Coogan tells me on the phone. There have been a few protests here, almost friendly in comparison to what has been going on elsewhere in Europe, in Africa, in Asia, in South America. Weak protests for abortion rights, against austerity, confusion regarding why a few wealthy white men were allowed to collapse a world economy and laugh about it and why none of them are in jail.

They do a lot of studies about humans and this inability to act. They lock men in rooms and give them buttons they are supposed to press until a light goes on. Only some of those buttons aren't wired to the light at all, and the button pushers sit there, wondering what they are doing wrong, why everyone else's light is going on except theirs. The scientists measure how long they sit there, pushing with no results, how long it takes them to get up and ask for help or declare this is bullshit. It's the fear that they are doing it wrong and will be corrected with a smirk that keeps them in their chairs.

They strap dogs down in front of an open door, and then they hurt them with electric shocks. Relentlessly. The dog struggles and struggles, trying to get to that doorway, to freedom, but the restraints hold him fast. This goes on so long that the dog gives up. This goes on so long that even after the restraints are removed the dogs don't bother to try to escape. Learned help-lessness.

When I read about the first experiment, the researchers made it clear that they explained to everyone the basic mecha-nism of the experiment after it was over, so that no one went home feeling like a failure. But I think about those few partici-pants whose metaphorical buttons were not attached to their metaphorical lights, those for whom nothing in our money-worshiping society was working out, if that stink of failure could not so easily be washed away. Like those days when you keep dying in the video game at the exact same place, not because there's a trick to it you haven't figured out yet, no, it's suddenly because you are a failure as a human being and you never get anything right and your life is just one long series of disaster after fucking disaster and that is just who you are as a person, isn't it? How many of those had to walk by the river on their way home and find the strength to say, "Not today"?

The dogs, no one says what happens to the dogs. I imagine some undomesticate themselves and have to be destroyed.

* * *

Maud believed in armed revolution, but she knew it wasn't just guns the Irish needed, it was new stories. Stories about who they were, where they came from, what they were capable of. Something to replace this long built-in tale of powerlessness and learned helplessness.

Maud was a woman of the stage, and at six feet tall with flaming red hair, she struck an iconic figure. In W. B. Yeats she found a powerful collaborator, as in thrall to the old Celtic tales as she was, the old pagan myths and stories of fairies and spirits. Yeats would write plays to revive these old storylines, stories of battles fought and won, of heroism and tragedy. Maud would appear on stage as the personification of Ireland or one of the great goddesses or heroines. She traveled the country giving speeches, and when she opened her mouth it was not her own voice that emerged, it was the voice of Ireland. She would stumble from the stage in a daze, unsure what she had said or how it went. She felt possessed. She made her body into an instrument for the nation to use to incite its people to resistance. To women in the Daughters of Erin, she lectured about the older stories of women, about Medb and Brigid and Morrigan. Women who were not just mothers and wives and daughters, dutiful all. Women who were warriors, women who were queens.

That was the draw of the Golden Dawn and the Theosophists and the other mystery cults and magic systems of the time. The women were not subservient, they were priestesses. They were part of the hierarchy. They could and did attain positions of power. And in the stories the women were not simply virginal conduits through which a divine-human hybrid could find life. They were goddesses and they were equal to the gods. They were creators, they brought war and love and rebirth. Women in these systems, they could fuck, they could have their voices heard, they could stand alongside their brothers.

But. It didn't take. Any of it. The armed struggle deteriorated into my god versus your god, men and women remain under the thumb of a patriarchal church, and while we can't blame Aleister Crowley for ruining magic for us, it's fun to try. Crowley, the only spiritual leader who thought, what's needed here is way more ego. Magic and ritual cannot sway the line between victory and defeat, but it can inspire the will to fight. It changes consciousness even if it does not change matter, and that is just as important. That is what new narratives do, they change consciousness by changing the story you tell yourself. That's what those idiotic materialists never understand. We are not slaves to unconscious drives unless we insist on believing that the subconscious is weaker or less important or dumber than our logical skills, if we neglect it and don't dive in. The important task is to understand and modify the stories that are holding sway. You can't bully the prerational with the rational. You need to communicate with it on its level: myth, ritual, symbol, metaphor. With magic.

The old stories in Maud's and W. B.'s time were too deeply

entrenched. There was an unwillingness to bring this all to light, the patriarchy, the Church, the complicity they played with their own subjugation. When Maud applied to join the Celtic Literary Society, she was told no women were allowed. When she tried to find the Ladies Land League to fight against illegal evictions of Irish tenants by British landowners, she found it had been disbanded by the all-male Land League.

There are no human rights if you're still arguing about who counts as human. It is so very difficult to bear the weight of powerlessness. Especially men, it seems, who were and are raised to believe they are the keepers of the world. When they find their worlds diminished, or fantastical, stealing ground from the others around them, even more powerless than they are, is a disappointing pattern.

Maud was not the Irish Joan of Arc she wanted to be, not unless you're defining her by the moment when the men beat her back.

* * *

The Irishman and I are walking to the movies together when he points toward the vacant building we are passing and says, "That used to be a Magdalene laundry."

I'm shocked, too shocked to say anything, so we keep walking. I had known about the laundries, where women were sentenced by courts or families to slavelike conditions of unpaid labor and abuse. Unfit women, needing to be punished for being willful or criminal or sexual. From what I've read, it seemed "raped" was a subcategory of "sexual" and was also deemed worthy of punishment. It took until 1996 for all the laundries to be closed. They were run by the Church, and under its watch the women in their care were sexually abused, physically tortured, and if any of them gave birth to a child in the institution, it was often put up for adoption without any say of the mother.

I had pictured these houses as existing far away in the countryside. I figured their locations would have had to be hidden, somewhere remote and approachable only by horseback or something. Otherwise, wouldn't women just climb the fence and fuck off? I know many did, but I mean, like all of them: wouldn't the women of Galway storm the barricades with torches and homemade explosives, freeing the Magdalene girls like Bastille prisoners? There should be heroic paintings of just that hanging in the Dublin National Gallery, eight feet tall.

(Why am I not overthrowing my own government? Why did Occupy Wall Street all decide just to go home? Why aren't we jailing our bankers, demanding economic justice, or at least creating our own parallel system of housing, health care, social safety nets, and food supplies? We are ruled by anxiety, too, but the source is corporations and advertising agencies, and our anxiety is soothed by psychopharamaceuticals and consumer goods.)

My mind is a tangle, and we sit in the dark and watch an Irish film about vampires. The vampires go to high school. On our way to the bar after, I yell about the movie instead of my own feelings of powerlessness and despair.

"Vampires in high school! Why do people keep telling this stupid fucking story?" My voice is actually raised, my hands are actually shaking with anger. "If you were fucking immortal, right? And you were forever in the body of a hot seventeen-year-old chick, would you go back to high school? To endlessly have to go to gym class? To deal with fucking mean girl cheerleaders your whole multicentury existence? And I was a cheerleader, so I know what I am saying. No. No you would fucking not. You would go seduce men and see the world and build a fucking empire. You would not go to algebra class."

Poor Irishman. He is gentle and crooked, and I met him at a bookstore. He was to be a scientist until his brain broke and all sorts of things crawled out of his unconscious. Now he needs meditation and silence to be okay, and I keep dragging him out because I need the company. I buy his beer, it is the least I can do, and he pulls biscuits he baked for me out of his rucksack.

"I'm sorry I yelled."

"That's all right."

We sit side by side in our booth, and neither one of us say the things we need to say.

* * *

"What's the name of your magazine again, dear?"

"It's called *Bookslut*."

"Ah! I'm a man with a lifelong interest in sluts."

When I saw how much pushback Tim Pat Coogan was getting for his book *The Famine Plot*, which details just how responsible England was for the 1.5 million deaths during the Famine, I knew I wanted to talk to him. I managed to get him on the phone. He was being accused of lying, of stirring up bad feelings against the British, of potentially restarting the whole IRA thing again, of whining about things that had happened so far in the past. These accusations were coming from his own countrymen.

"You've got to remember that a lot of the problem was caused because England had taken away our government at the time," he tells me as I open up the discussion of the links between the Famine then and the financial crisis now.

"In our lifetime, in the last few years only, due to the profligacy of our government, and our bankers, and the corrupt civil servants who didn't monitor what was happening or didn't do anything about it if they did, we've again lost our sovereignty. Ireland can't spend a dime without the say-so of the IMF. We have legislation, insolvency legislation, and it lays down criteria for what you can spend on each family. There are lessons to be learned from the Famine. This thing, too, that was developed during the Famine and continues, 'learned helplessness.' There's nothing you can do, so you just submit. Well, the combination of the effects of the Famine and the authoritarian religion we had, two colonial structures we had, Mother England and Mother Church, it's left us subject to authority. And very reluctant to take stands or have self-belief. As a result, no one is doing anything about the terrible crisis."

After we've hung up, my brain keeps going back to this line in *The Famine Plot*. "Providence, the divine will, was declared to have a large bearing on the subject, as it generally does when the rich debate the poor, or the strong confront the weak. It was an era in which in America the indigenous Americans were going down before a similar doctrine: Manifest Destiny."

The fated argument soothes the weak as well as justifying the strong. It absolves the sin of inaction. And it protects us from the disappointment of at best an incomplete revolution and at worst utter failure.

I wonder if Maud knew she was going to fail. She helped to achieve the compromise of Home Rule, but the change in consciousness and narrative she fought so hard for, those still, all these years later, have not come about.

*   *   *

There's supposed to be all of this glamour and romance in the story of Yeats and Gonne, but I find the dynamic disturbing. When they met, Yeats recalled her as "a classical impersonation of the Spring; the Virgilian commendation 'She walks like a goddess' made for her alone." Maud did not remember him; she thought they met at a party somewhere else. W. B. described her as a dozen different virginal goddesses and nymphs while she was having a sexual affair with a married man and giving birth to her illegitimate son. W. B. proclaimed how intimately he understood her, how perfect they would be together, how very much in love he was, and yet when Maud told him her real life circumstances, he was horrified and repulsed.

One could say she was his muse—there certainly are volumes of his writings inspired by her—but she moved around too much to be anyone's muse. Muses are supposed to lie prone, allow the poetry to wash over them. It was his inner image of her that was his inspiration, and she had very little to do with that. She was smart enough never to turn his vapor into flesh. His delicate constitution would not have been able to stand the shock.

"Give up this tragic struggle and live a peaceful life," Yeats wrote to her in one of his innumerable proposals, missing the fact that for Maud the struggle was all.

Her response: "The world should thank me for not marrying you."

It was Yeats who brought Gonne to the Golden Dawn. He was heavily involved in its doings and with its members, and he thought its quiet study and stability would be good for Gonne, and by that I of course mean it would entwine their souls ever more tightly and keep her from straying too far.

Becoming a member of the Golden Dawn required patience and deep learning. As in any other mystery cult, there were progressive steps, and moving from one level to another required proving your level of knowledge, the acquisition of certain skills, and passing tests from those more advanced than you. The Golden Dawn was built on both the Kabbalah and Rosicrucianism, and there were Hebrew alphabets to learn, numerology, tarot cards, invocations, rituals, planetary symbols, talismans, divinations. The amount of information was enormous, and it took years for devotees to move up the ranks.

Maud Gonne had no use for any of it, and when she realized how long it was going to take before anyone taught her any real magic, she bailed. She did not have time for this shit (and she found the mystical woo-woo people in the order insufferable). She had a dead son to resurrect.

Her first son, Georges, had been sickly for some time, and when he finally succumbed Maud blamed herself for having been away so frequently. She had put her fight for Ireland and her political work ahead of him, she was afraid, and her guilt and grief at his death was shattering. And so she came up with this plan for his resurrection and promised herself she would do a better job this time.

On All Hallows' Eve, she and Georges's father went to the grave where he was buried, and they had sex in a vault as part of some unknown ritual—probably half homemade and half from some book she had found. Either way, she became pregnant that night and her never-ending guilt was healed. She gave birth to her daughter Iseult / resurrected son Georges the next year.

While Yeats was skrying and receiving visions of his past lives and channeling the spirit of the times to help his poetry, Maud's interest in the occult was more deeply personal. Yeats was a tourist, Maud lived in the underworld. Or at least had an involuntary access that she couldn't quite control. That's handy if you have someone you want to bring back from the dead, but not so handy for doing things like going to the grocery store. You're in the produce aisle just trying to pick out some radishes, and suddenly you're picking up messages from the beyond. Weeks before Maud's father's death, she saw his funeral in exact detail in her dreams, and then was horrified to see it replay before her in the real world. From a young age she was haunted by a woman shrouded in a gray shawl, and the woman appeared to her as often when she was awake as when she was asleep. Paintings moved and conversed with her. Spirits and demons were right under the surface of her reality.

We could diagnose her, sure. Any woman today with a similar reality, no matter how high functioning, would be saddled with the sentence of schizophrenia and given large doses of antipsychotics. Or labeled a liar and a charlatan. I prefer to think of Maud as just living in a world with slightly shifted veils. Just as she preferred to think of the body of Iseult as containing the soul of Georges.

* * *

I go out looking for a spell. A spell for what, though. A spell for healing? I could use healing, that wonderfully vague word, another stupid story we tell ourselves about our lives. Recovery. Healing. A Journey of Self-Discovery. All so very inward facing, but occasionally your insides demand your attention, the point is just to remember to look out again. I want my spirit to feel like my body felt at the Roman baths in Baden-Baden, a little memory I keep in my pocket. At the very least I would like a good night's sleep that doesn't require whiskey to get there.

In the basement of the shopping center, next to a scented candle shop that could have bodies buried under their floorboards, you'd never know, is a small New Age store. There are angel divination cards, a rack of crystals, only half of which match their labels. There are books on healing journeys, on communication with angels and fairies, packs of incense. Buddhas carved out of jade for non-Buddhists. Ganeshes carved out of quartz for non-Hindus.

I find an open Goddess divination card deck, and I flip through it. Morrigan, who was the battle warrior goddess, the goddess of strife and of revenge, she's here to tell you how to make change in your life. Not how to rip off the head of your enemy oppressor and drink his blood as his brothers in battle watch, but how to have the confidence to ask for that raise.

She's painted as super-busty, of course, all leather corset and dark raven consort.

This store is the equivalent of an SSRI treatment, allowing you to not notice how fucking insane the world you are walking into actually is. It tells you that you are responsible only for yourself, that your little world is the only world that matters. One of the reasons Gonne was disgusted with her Golden Dawn cohorts was their response to the building violence of the age: to contemplate and to pray. Gonne proclaimed herself a pacifist, but in times of war, she said, you pick up the gun and kill the enemy, you do not kneel before them and hope the spirit world will intervene.

I bet Morrigan misses Maud Gonne. I bet she wishes people would make offerings of the cut-out heart of the occupier, rather than fresh-cut flowers and incense. I bet she wishes people would ask for more rivers of blood and fewer inner senses of self-worth.

I walk back through the small downtown area to meet the Irishman for a drink. The pedestrian walkway is a big *It's a Small World after All* presentation for the tourists, who still flock to Ireland despite the gloomy economic situation. The cobblestones are scrubbed clean, musicians and singers busk for coins along the way; there are "traditional" Irish pubs with "traditional" Irish music pouring out of the open windows, advertising the "traditional" Irish breakfast, only five pounds on weekdays, shops selling "traditional" woolen sweaters and little stuffed leprechauns for the kids.

You only have to move a few blocks eastward or westward to see boarded-up storefronts and sad old men who look like they haven't left the off-track betting shop for going on five years now. There are signs pasted up, someone who has obviously thoroughly studied the Irish constitution and found that income tax is actually not required, and he's trying to spread the news. STOP PAYING INCOME TAX, his black-and-white printouts scream, with a little gibberish underneath about statutes and how they can't hurt you if you don't pay.

I meet the Irishman in the back of a bar, he is drinking a pint, I'm drinking a whiskey neat. The table next to us are Americans, and they hear an Irish accent, perhaps the only one in this place that doesn't belong to the bartender, and they strike up a conversation with my friend about how beautiful it is here, how natural and how green. They are from Chicago, they are both lawyers. He is boisterous (drunk) and friendly, he looks like he is going to hug everyone who passes his way. She sullenly pokes at her smartphone, looking up with interest only when I tell her I used to live in Chicago. She realizes we know none of the same people and she goes back to her phone.

He talks about his downtown condo, his high-powered job. I think he uses that phrase *high-powered*, it's hard to tell, the whiskey is going into an empty stomach. They are on their honeymoon, driving around Ireland. "I thought it would be depressing, because, you know. But it's not, everyone has been so friendly." They're Irish, somehow, way back, they say. They're cloudy on how far back and how Irish, but they're here to find their roots.

"Are you Irish?" he asks me.

"No, my family were Cromwell loyalists. It's why I'm drinking Bushmills." He looks blank. "Protestant landowners. I'm here to pay penance and give them all of my money in exchange for their whiskey." I pull on the Irishman's sleeve and tell him I need fried food in my stomach or things are going to go weird.

All of this terrible need for Irish roots, as if being Irish were just an endless St. Patrick's Day parade of green beer and green vomit. Kiss the Blarney Stone for a gift of the gab. I have read a hundred travel writers exploring Ireland and explaining their deep connection to the land. I mean, me too. I am that awful as well. When I was nineteen this was where I ran to when I ran from college and family and my expectations for what my life would be like, with some vague notion that my family was Irish. We're not.

At least we are not the only ones, Maud did it, too, pretending at Irish. Lecturing Yeats on how he wasn't Irish enough, not as Irish as her British self. An outsider leading a land into rebellion, or trying to.

Now that we are all so in love with our identities and our identifying marks, our gender, our race, our sexuality, our nationality, our blood type, now that we rank how oppressed we are, which combination of demographics possesses the most privilege, who is scoring highest today on the pain scale, we would bristle at the thought of an outsider speaking for us. Male feminists are shouted down about their privilege, allies are humiliated for being tourists, "not knowing what it is like." You can't show appreciation for a culture without being accused of appropriation. And yet who but an outsider can see our way out of our own private thornbushes, not being entangled herself?

You can love a place and not be able to live there. After leaving at nineteen, when my six-month visa ran out, I thought, *I will come back. I will be Irish in one way if not in another.* But for all of the talk of the burst housing bubble and huge numbers of houses sitting empty and unfinished, the rents in the city are still shockingly high, and it is still expensive and difficult to be a middle- to lower-class woman of childbearing age in this place. Even if you're self-employed and somewhat immune to the waxing and waning of the job market. It is why the emigration rates are the highest they have been since the Famine. It's hard to say who is betraying whom here, the nation betraying its young people or the young people betraying their nation. By not rebelling, not paralleling, not taking care of each other rather than fleeing for high ground, fighting for little scraps of land in Germany, in the US, in England. The suicide rates are also very high, although only unofficially. Suicide is still taboo here, and death certificates can be faked.

Maud couldn't live here either; mostly she was in France. She was a presence here, but she was smart enough to keep her belongings elsewhere. With her gunrunning and spying, not to mention her illegitimate-child bearing, she would not have made it here. She came and went, visiting Yeats in Dublin with her Great Dane and her winged hat, freaking out the locals and embodying Ireland. And then she could return to France and be a human and a lover and a mother and a black magician.

It's too bad there was no spell big enough to break the hold of England over Ireland. Today we would need one equally big to break the hold of the IMF and these sick ideas we have about what success looks like, what "a good life" is. I don't know how many black cats would have to be killed silently for that to work. It hasn't shown up in any of my grimoires.

* * *

One morning I wake up in my damp room, and I am myself again. Somehow. I don't question it, I just remind myself how few of these days we get, those of us whose neurons are a mess, days when your arms and legs do what you want them to do, days when your first impulse upon waking is not to cry, days when you remember how to want things. I have this apartment for another week, but I pack up my things and arrange elaborate travel to take me to Budapest for a five-day rest. I need goulash, I think. I need sun, more sun than is allocated per person in Ireland. I need plum brandy and bathhouses and art deco buildings. I know what I want, and what I want is to leave.

Lausanne / Igor Stravinsky

"You know they've hollowed out some of the mountains, don't you?"

It sounds like some sort of marvelous conspiracy theory, but the Irish writer I'm talking to is of reasonable sanity despite the extensive collection of swords that line his walls and almost cut off my toes when I stumbled around in the dark looking for the bathroom early one morning and laid my hand on the wrong thing to try to steady myself.

"They have bomb shelters for something like 95 percent of their population. You know how many Americans would be saved by shelters in a nuclear attack? Less than 5 percent."

"Is that something we still have to worry . . ."

His wife breaks in. "And the bridges in and out of the country are wired with explosives, so they can isolate themselves in a minute in case of attack."

At the time of the conversation, it sounded like they had both read a *New Yorker* article and retained the wrong information, but a little poking around proved them accurate, with only a little exaggeration. Switzerland is ready, at all times, to cut itself off from the rest of the world. A country that declares neutrality had better be able to enforce that neutrality, and Switzerland most certainly can, from its mandatory conscripted army to its collapsible bridges—not actually wired with explosives, although there is a plan in place for every bridge built on how to bring it down in an instant. New construction projects may not be planned out on the foundations of paranoia anymore, but much of the country's existing infrastructure was put in place when they were.

It's not as if the impulse has died, it seems only to have shifted. Sharing a border with Germany will make a girl nervous, sure, but the extremes the country has gone to, and the whole populace nodding their heads and saying yes, that seems reasonable, let's hollow out some mountains, I'll vote for that, reveals something a little more internal. And when we are in the grips of an unconscious urge, we can stop one behavior but another simply forms in its place, manifesting the same urge wearing a different dress.

So when Switzerland makes the international news these days, it's for banning the construction of minarets while comparing the shape of the structure to a nuclear missile, or for strictly limiting the number of immigrants, or for some other gesture out of line with the European talking point of inclusivity and fluid borders. Switzerland knows: there is more than one way to build a fortress.

* * *

No tunnels collapse nor bridges fall as I pass from the German border into Switzerland, and so I guess that means they do not see me as a threat. I have been in Switzerland before, always while in an emotional lull. This is a very good place to come when one is falling apart; the solidity of the place, the physicality of those mountains that snugly close you in, becomes something of an emotional exoskeleton.

I have met with a bit of luck: a family of three is heading off on travels and has invited me to borrow their farmhouse up from Lake Geneva while they are away. They are strangers to me, I've never met them. But she is a writer, and Facebook can be a small place sometimes if you ask for help. The train, however, has mysteriously stalled two stops away from my destination. The doors hang open, the audio system is silent, and everyone carries on as normal as the minutes tick by. The only sound is the rain hammering on the roof of the train station.

After twenty minutes I dig the scrap of paper with Michelle's phone number out of my pocket to tell her I will be late. "Get off the train," she tells me as she hops in her car. I do, and stare back at the passengers, all still sitting silently. She pulls up.

"Did they say why?"

"No, there weren't any announcements."

"Suicide on the tracks, maybe. Otherwise they give you a reason."

I must remind myself to leave this country eventually. If one stays too long and the exoskeleton is not shed, it can crush the growing creature under it. All of my favorite Swiss writers were mad.

Michelle and her family greet me with wine and pasta and a cozy, warm house. While quietly dripping rainwater on their floor, I nod through instructions on how to build a fire to heat the house, how to walk to the train station, how not to spook the cows, as well as the daughter's explanation about all of her princess dolls, and then I crawl into bed. When I wake, they have left for the airport and I am alone. I am alone with my suitcase in a farmhouse a twenty-minute train ride from Lausanne, where I don't speak the language and I don't know anyone. The family sweetly left me the keys to their car in case of an emergency, but I don't even have a driver's license. The rain continues, hard and cold, and the country roads are a washed-out slick of mud. I'm not sure how to get groceries. Maybe this should have been thought through.

* * *

Lausanne was once an intellectual capital, attracting great thinkers such as Rousseau and Voltaire. Today it is a haven for those who love water skiing, swimming and sailing.

Lausanne tourism website

There are many advantages to fortresses, as long as you scan as insider. Many philosophers, dictators, writers, artists, spies, musicians, dancers, and composers have taken shelter in Switzerland while their own countries failed to keep it together. When nations insisted that their poets head off to war, many poets went to Switzerland and lived through it instead.

Igor Stravinsky showed up with his family in 1914, hoping to get himself out of the way of the war. He had been living in France, and although he was still young, in his thirties, he had a trio of great successes behind him: *Firebird*, *Petrushka*, *Rite of Spring*. He had the ballet company Ballets Russes to produce his work, and an audience that loved and hated him, and he could do exactly as he pleased.

But now he found his career interrupted. World War I would cut him off from the Ballets Russes and the Parisian orchestras—most musicians found themselves enlisted, willingly or not. It's curious, looking back now, to see how enthusiastically so many men went off to war that time round, for such a nonsensical cause. It is difficult to conjure up, even in the imagination, so much trust in the government, so much glory in mutilation and bloodshed. But their naiveté met up with mustard gas and artillery, changing the cheery faces of soldiers forever.

Stravinsky detested upheaval of any kind, so much so that he even shrank at the description of his music as "revolutionary." He did not want to cheer on the forces or participate in the war effort, he wanted a quiet place to write his music. He and his family went to Switzerland, where they could be sheltered during the years of tumult, and they moved into a house on the shores of Lake Geneva, near Lausanne. It would give them a bit of stability, and they wouldn't have to keep shuffling around as the front of the war shifted around Europe.

But the Russian Revolution that followed three years later would isolate him further, as many Russian émigrés went running back home to assist the rebuilding of the nation, and he was cut off financially from his family's estate. He stayed where he was, forced to start over without the collaborators he had worked with for the entirety of his career and without means of support. He found his world reduced to his small house with his blank notebooks and his piano. It was time to begin again.

* * *

We can be grateful to Switzerland for keeping Stravinsky safe, for keeping James Joyce safe, and W. Somerset Maugham, too. We can approve of their guarded nature when the outside world goes all turmoil and muddle.

And when it doesn't. When the barbarians are not at the gate. When there is no one just on the other side of that hill, plotting your destruction. Is your guard up or down? And what if it is up, always up? What task can we give that guard to do, carrying as he does all of the wounds of battles past and all of those very specific skills honed? Because left to his own devices, that is a person who knows only one thing, and that is who is in and who is out. How to tell, how to mark them. That guard, he'll be out there discriminating, no matter what the geopolitical climate; it is all he knows how to do.

* * *

I have always enjoyed my time in Switzerland and found the Swiss to be polite and welcoming, but I am aware that is in part because I meet their requirements: I am white, I come from a nation that is an ally, I am an intellectual and financially self-sufficient. In the French part I may not be able to communicate in their native tongue, but I know enough of the language to apologize and ingratiate myself while asking if they would not mind terribly speaking English with me.

Of course I have found Switzerland to be hospitable—I am instantly on their list of those to be included. I wonder how many adjustments to my identity would be required before they started to sense me as other and shut the gates and barred my passage.

I am welcomed, but I am not one of them. Strange, then, that I feel like I fit in visually only in Europe. My strange face, all angles and bone: from the left it reads Slavic and from the right Celtic. When I was twenty-eight, I looked up on a train going through Frankfurt and for the first time noticed that my face had a context, it fit in somewhere. I was no longer in a lifelong game of One of These Things Is Not like the Others. Even in my home state the first words out of someone's mouth is Where You From. When I say Here, there is blankness or a jerk of the head back and to the right. Nah. I mean, Where You Born. Here.

When I travel through Europe, my face reads as Here. Here is assumed. Then I open my mouth and out comes discordance and no one knows where to put me. And that first impression, of One of Us, is hard to shake, that visual code takes dismantling. Because I can sit and speak English with a native, in my American accent, and the Swiss will still ask if I'm from near here. No, I'm not Swiss. Then a jerk of the head back and to the right.

It gets me by in Europe. The assumption of competence, the assumption of belonging. I am the person always approached for directions. You can glide through with a pass like this, particularly if you know when to keep your mouth shut.

* * *

Anna Göldi was a servant woman who was probably sleeping with her boss. Not in a oh, how scandalous kind of way, more like an *I don't want to die on the streets cold and hungry* kind of arrangement.

Something happened. Doubtless we'll never really know what, it is not like anyone was going to listen to a poor servant woman. Maybe she fought back. Maybe she threatened to tell. Whatever it was, after seventeen years in the employment of Dr. Johann Jakob Tschudi, he suddenly accused her of being a witch. Tschudi's daughter started coughing up needles, magically hidden by Göldi in the girl's milk, or maybe placed in the girl's body by otherworldly means.

Under torture she confessed, as one does. And she was executed—beheaded—even though the daughter survived the spitting of pins. The death sentence was probably just some reflexive twitch at that point; the witch hunts in Switzerland had been particularly thorough and bloody. Some sources say that in certain areas, more than one village was thoroughly purged until not a single adult woman remained.

Göldi was the last, though. The last woman executed for witchcraft in Europe, although certainly not the last accused or the last found guilty. Britain had cases up into the twentieth century, but courts after this did manage to find some restraint. This was 1782, after the Enlightenment, after the deaths of Voltaire and Rousseau and the other great thinkers, way after anyone should have heard accusations of witchcraft and thought *Okay, well, let's get the red-hot pincers and see what we can find out.*

That guard, he needs someone to give him something else to do.

The rain will not stop. I am running out of food, and so my meals become increasingly random. "Help yourself to whatever" was the final remark tossed over a shoulder, so I do to avoid having to walk down the muddy hill and wait under an umbrella for the train into town. My lunch is a slice of bread with peanut butter, a knob of cheese, an apple, and a cup of tea. Dinner looks like it is going to be microwave popcorn and a sausage.

There are Alps out there somewhere, but they are cloaked by the low clouds. The clouds hem in the countryside. I can see only as far as the neighboring farm, and I can hear this farm's cows in the barn, ringing their bells and letting loose with the occasional cooped-up bellow (I feel your pain, ladies). The farmers' son wanders by in wellies, with his broad shoulders and thick hands and his easily startled virginal floor gaze. He looks like a gentleman I know. He could, in fact, be his doppelgänger. "That means you have to jump him," the gentleman writes to me, always the romantic.

Mostly I take baths while reading Elizabeth Smart and other tales of emotional devastation, and then I build fires in the furnace in preparation for the next bath. The barn attaches, so I can carry in new wood without slopping through the mud, and the wood is refilled weekly by the farmers' son. He chops it, back there, in a sweaty shirt I bet, mud down the front of his jeans, I bet if I took him out a glass of water . . . The cat I am supposed to be tending brings in the outside world for me, tracking in mud and cow shit and howling at me for her half-empty food bowl before disappearing for another twenty-four hours. I feed her and mop up the mud and try not to think about how this waterphobic beast is more tolerant of the downpour than I am.

At some point, this will be beautiful. At some point, my

kingdom will encompass more than this house and more than the same four outfits I've been wearing for a year now. It's been five hours, I can have another bath now, right? Right.

* * *

Stravinsky often had to have the limits of his job mapped out before he could get to work; he couldn't be wholly free save in bondage.

BORIS DE SCHLOEZER

The question is not so much how Stravinsky revolutionized his musical style while in Switzerland. There are many, many books already on the subject; his time in Switzerland, spent without his collaborators, without an orchestra, and yet still producing and performing music, his switch from orchestral to chamber music, the way the deprivation actually inspired him, the way he was able to break further from his Russian roots and bring a more European and American flavor to his work—it's all been written about before. As a Russian writer asked me before I left, "Why are you writing about Stravinsky in Switzerland? Everyone writes about Stravinsky in Switzerland. Even I have written about Stravinsky in Switzerland."

There really isn't a composer who has been written about more. Even Stravinsky wrote about Stravinsky in Switzerland; he was one of the few composers able to clearly articulate his own thinking and process. He's a favorite subject because his music thinks, and you have to think along with it to bring it in. It's also deeply emotional and intuitive, it's not a theoretical exercise. That combination of soul and brain is rare. You have the initial body-shaking, spine-electrifying experience where all of your cells start humming in key, but then you want to figure out what this marvelous man is doing and your brain goes to work.

I am dissatisfied reading and thinking about Stravinsky's life because it doesn't align with the music. The music seems wholly separate. He once told a friend that the first notes of a piece always come from God, his job is to chase down the others and give them form. We are so accustomed to thinking of artists as being tied to their work through their lives: the music or the book or the painting is an expression of what is happening in their existence. And yet with Stravinsky it seems entirely other. The structures and the restrictions, those seem imposed by biography: what instrument is around at the time, et cetera. But the notes that structure is filled with, they seem unattached. Free-floating and sure, yes, divine.

Because when I listen to *Petrushka*, I don't feel the connection to Stravinsky the person, where he was in his life, the work with Diaghilev, the history as Rimsky-Korsakov's student, the ambitious young man, not even thirty, trying to prove himself after his debut *Firebird* was an instant success. Not in the way one can align, say, *Portrait of the Artist as a Young Man* with James Joyce or *Don Giovanni* with Mozart. With Stravinsky it feels separate, as each piece of music feels separate from the one that came before and the one that follows. There is no dot dot dot, nothing that clings from one project to the next, no one big idea that he is trying to work out, the way artists sometimes get stuck and simply express the same thing over and over again, beautifully to be sure, but retreading the same ground, just from a different angle each time. Every time Stravinsky went to work he created wholly new beings. And those beings are not tied down, they are free to roam the earth without him.

So, no. I'm not so interested in thinking about Stravinsky's life in Switzerland, I don't want to go stomping through his house with my muddy sneakers, I don't want to sit in his favorite café and try to align myself with his spirit. I am interested in thinking through a thought. This idea of restriction. Of how

Stravinsky flourished under its weight, while it kills other artists dead. How do you keep working when all seems lost? When you are forced to break with the past and start anew?

In 1918 Stravinsky debuted one of his most successful and popular works, *Historie du soldat*, in Lausanne. He had been used to working with orchestras, but this story of a soldier's deal with the Devil was played on a violin, a double bass, a cornet, a trombone, a clarinet, a bassoon, and percussion. That was what was around. He wrote it with the Swiss writer C. F. Ramuz, because that was who was around. The piece is filled with adopted forms, a waltz, a tango, ragtime, all distinctively made Stravinskian. And then those drums, at the end, that stop your heart.

Maybe it helps to think that the first notes, the first idea, that first splash of color, come from outside of yourself. The genii and the muses, they are infinite, they are timeless. They can't come into this world without the structure put into place first. The mortal cannot grasp the reality of the infinite; we need limitations. Our expression of the divine will always be, has to be, a flawed reduction of the pure potential.

But also, just as we set up the walls within which the divine beings can come and play, the muses can work only with what the artist has to offer. The job of the artist should not only be to take dictation, it should be to make oneself as large a canvas as possible, to constantly be pushing at one's boundaries. Stravinsky did that by playing with all sorts of new forms, by traveling constantly and meeting things that were strange and new with enthusiasm. By acknowledging his limitations. he could work at unbuilding them. The physical restrictions of money and place and instrumentation, then, were just paradoxical tools of expansion.

How that act will be done, the expansion, will be different every time. Traveling around the world or quiet study or political engagement, it doesn't matter. It gives the genii temporarily inhabiting your body something new to do. And not to expand is to insult the muses. To believe you are the creator of your own world is to dishonor the divine. When you believe that you are in charge, that you are not in a collaboration every time you sit alone at your desk, it's no wonder what comes from your pen is so earthbound and weighty. No wonder the muses turn up their noses.

* * *

This is my entire world: one carry-on-sized suitcase and one backpack and one dark blue sweatshirt dress / security blanket. The number of books varies depending on how long it's been since there was an English-language bookstore nearby. One nice cocktail dress and one good pair of heels for emergency opera; one pair of jeans, new, after the others ripped in the ass and had to be quickly replaced; three T-shirts of varying sleeve-lengths; the mysteriously dwindling underwear supply; two sundresses; one sweater; one leather jacket; one pair of sneakers and one pair of ballet flats; one bag of cosmetics and toiletries; one black leather clutch, carrying necklaces wrapped in toilet paper.

I treasure and despise each of these items. I know their exact contours, their weight, their size when folded and their size when rolled. Everything here is just a little bit larger and a little bit heavier than I would prefer. The totality of my possessions is carefully considered so that I can lift the bags over my head without assistance, no matter how sick or hung over I might be. There are emergency stashes of necessities that I try to forget are there so they are not used up: emergency tampons, emergency aspirin, emergency Irish breakfast tea.

In one month it will be one year on the road with this exact suitcase, although I did get to switch out clothes once from boxes held in storage. That was a glorious day, the promise of new outfits, of making myself new all over again. The delight of that wore off the third day of wearing the same shirt in a row. But oh, what a day.

I am simultaneously covetous for objects and despising of possessions now. I want a house, a house that stays in one place and doesn't wander off, where I get to decide on the furnishings and the artwork and the colors of the wall and the books on the shelves and there will be a kettle, definitely, I will definitely not have to boil water in a saucepan to make my morning tea. I will fill it full of things. I will have so many outfits I can discard each one after its debut. I will have mountains of high heels. Bookshelves full of just high heels in every color and every height, a library of shoes. Heels that have not been repaired three times already because the little nub was yanked off by a cobblestone street, because the sole wore through, because disembarking from a taxi wrenched the heel loose. And a separate library, full of books, books that I do not have to carry on my body, weighing me down; they will stay in their place, carried only from room to room and only one at a time. Every book or every subject matter, every type of book, a book to satisfy every whim and interest, every book I have ever wanted to read at any moment in my life: they will be within reach. Maybe I will also have some plants.

And yet when I think about buying things, and putting them all in the same place, and being around them, it just feels like another way to be weighed down. So I pet the wonderfully frilly blouse that does not match anything else in my suitcase; I would need to buy a pencil skirt maybe, or perhaps these slate blue slacks, which do not go with my shoes now that I think about it, but those pink kitten heels in the corner, maybe they are on sale . . . I leave the boutique in the same sweater I have worn now for a month, and I take the train back out to the farm.

* * *

Stravinsky was approached by Columbia Records after the war, after he left Switzerland for Paris, to record some music for them. At the time the 78 rpm disc could hold about three minutes of sound on each side, and so Stravinsky decided to create a whole new piece, one that would consist of three-minute segments, so that it would not be awkwardly chopped up as the listener switched over the disk.

The result is *Serenade in A for Piano*, a four-part take on German *Nachtmusik*. Each segment is distinct, with a wholly different structure, and yet they all "revolve about an axis of sound that happened to be the note 'A,'" as he explained in his autobiography.

I saw it performed once, by a Russian pianist, his entire body taking on Stravinsky's birdlike qualities. The quick jabs of the arms, the bobbing of the head and body, the beak of the nose inches from the keys.

At the time Stravinsky was writing *Serenade* he was touring America, excited by the jazz music he took in there and incorporating its rhythms and structures into his work. While other classical fetishists were despairing at the cold anarchy that was the rise of jazz and ragtime, Stravinsky was one of the few embracing it. And that arm-crossed refusal of most composers meant that audiences dwindled, notational music lost its power, composers were mostly thought of as high-minded buffoons, not geniuses. As the audience deserted the music, and composers started writing mostly for each other and less for people, the music started to become more cerebral, insular. The audience reduced further, and even they were regarded as high-minded buffoons. Now the divinities have moved on as composers bang notes down on paper in mathematical orders to bare-bones audiences, and the muses all went to go live in David Bowie's house.

With a strict admittance policy you're never sure who is getting accidentally turned away at the door.

* * *

When the rain eventually stops, the Alps reemerge. I can get groceries again, although rather than take the train into the city, I walk down the mountain I am living on, fill my backpack full of meats and fruits and bottles of wine in the little village market, and then hike back up. The neighbor's dog barked fiercely the first time I passed by her house, and I played submissive with the downturned gaze, the bowed head, the deflection of my path. The second time she came up, tail wagging, to say hello. I laid down my pack and scratched her head and she leaned her body into mine. But when I raised my hand too quickly, moving to swat a fly, she bolted, jerking backwards, frightened. Oh, you poor dear, I tell her. I know what precedes that movement, what comes in the year before that flinch becomes reflex.

The dog, the cows, they are my conversation partners. Cows are wonderful to talk to, they carefully consider your every word. Now that spring has lazily pulled off its slicker and wellies, the cows are let loose in the yard and I can watch them for hours. It is hard to believe such massive beasts can frolic, and yet on their first day to pasture in a long time they do. They leap—a little, they are awfully earthbound; they race and skid in the mud. They fascinate me, the way they move, the way they rub up against one another to say hello. The way once they lie down their entire world is contained in a few inches around their bodies, as long as they can absorb the sunlight through their thick hide and as long as they can reach a little grass if they crane their neck so they don't have to stand up again. And the ducking of their heads and the ringing of their bells. One heifer will occasionally try to mount another but then get confused about what exactly is supposed to happen next, and then drop off the other's back. I try to play them Stravinsky out my window, but they seem to prefer the Guns N' Roses.

I want for nothing, out here. Not even loneliness can find me when the sun is out and the cows come up to the fence to say hello when I leave on my morning walk. The lover is back in my inbox, head bowed and living in his own guest room. We write, black type on a computer screen being safer than seeing his face and hearing his voice over Skype. But even then I can let that have its own place, I don't have to carry my sorrow up and down the mountain.

I'm running out of money, but I can read tarot cards over Skype for extra cash, there will always be someone who is in need of a new story to tell themselves about their life, and I can turn that bit of money into steak and mushroom pie (sorry, ladies) with a bit of effort. For the first time I can see that the things I have lost—my apartment, my circle of friends, the fantasy of my lover, a significant percentage of my income—were not necessary. I don't have to miss them. It's a choice. Here, the paltry contents of my life seem full and rich.

* * *

It's been a while since I've had a stereo and not just my laptop and cheap headphones, and I am taking the opportunity to fill my head and the house with Arrigo Boito's *Mefistofele*. It is his only opera. It is beautiful, but curious. Unearthly and strange, a little feline in the way the music slinks around the farmhouse. It was poorly received—I guess that is the correct phrase. Boito insisted on conducting the orchestra himself, despite his total lack of experience in doing such a thing. It was a disaster. Riots broke out, much like they did at the premiere of Stravinsky's *Rite*, although not because it was so Ziggy Stardust that its audience fought against it. There were riots because it was a mess. It only lasted two performances, and Boito never finished another opera, although his unwritten operas sometimes visit me in my dreams.

Boito came forty years before Stravinsky, and yet they are also separated by their output. What is the difference between an artist with a few high points and an artist with a career? Surely it's something more than a matter of character, or a matter of where Saturn is placed in their chart. There are artists who seem to be able to create only under the most ideal conditions, and ideal conditions are the most fleeting of things. It is so easy to get distracted by fame or a baby or an indifferent public.

We are forever trying to cultivate whatever that difference is—grit, perseverance, character. We design school curricula now on the idea that this is something that can be taught. Is it something inherent in a person, just something they are born with, or can we learn to live and thrive under ideal conditions? Can we all learn to sprout up like weeds, to accept our limitations with grace? When the world puts you into a tiny cell, how can you learn to make something out of the furnishings, rather than just gazing longingly out the barred window?

The most striking thing about *Soldat*, Stravinsky's Swiss chamber piece, is that every instrument is allowed to be itself. The cornet is not trying to be an oboe. He doesn't hammer the bassoon down to fit the part of a flute. Nothing is being used as a poor substitute for the things he really wishes he had. He is willing to look at what is available, evaluate their properties, and work within the constraints. There is no hissyfit about a grand vision, he does not waste his time on the ideal. He trusts the mundane to transcend. He works in the world. He forgives the clarinet for not being a cello.

We all must forgive our clarinet for not being a cello.

* * *

Of course it wasn't only the orchestra and the money and the rest of Europe that Stravinsky was cut off from while he was in Switzerland. It was Diaghilev.

Sergei Diaghilev was a beautiful monster. He was the magician, the person who pulled together ordinary materials and from them created the extraordinary. From almost nothing (certainly very little money) he created one of the most influential art movements of the twentieth century. His little ballet company influenced art, music, dance, fashion, design, and literature for an entire century. He made legends out of nobodies (Nijinsky, Stravinsky) and wooed legends to work on the pay scale of nobodies (Chanel, Picasso).

Stravinsky was a young man in his twenties whose outsized ambitions could not fit inside his scrawny little frame when Diaghilev chose him to compose *Firebird*. Choosing was perhaps Diaghilev's greatest gift, his ability to look at someone unpromising and unmade and see instead all that was yet to come. It was as if he stood outside of time and could see who would fit, who needed intervention, who needed to crash into whom. His collaborators both adored and despised him for this manipulation. They hated their reliance on him, and the way he slyly always made sure they were aware of how much of their lives they owed to him.

Firebird made Stravinsky a star. It was his first full work, his first time in Paris, and his first taste of celebrity. And he owed it all to Diaghilev. Certainly Stravinsky was grateful, and certainly gratitude can be an instrument of enslavement. It was a dy-

namic that suited Diaghilev and one that he abused with all of
his collaborators, until a sudden severing would cause the other
to spin out, away from Diaghilev's orbit, cursing his very name.

It was a fruitful arrangement for Stravinsky. If *Firebird* made
him a star, *Petrushka* made him a genius, and *Rite of Spring*
made him notorious. And after the riot, the one that left Stravinsky holding on to the back of Nijinsky's costume backstage
to keep him from running out to yell at the audience to shut the
fuck up and caused Nijinsky's mother to faint, the one that has
been mythologized and directly corresponds to what we think
when we think about Stravinsky, Diaghilev turned to Stravinsky
and said, "Exactly what I wanted."

It was fruitful, but there is a moment when those arrangements cease to be so. A genius who feels grateful to their pro-
ducer or manager is someone who doesn't understand or believe in their own power. But Diaghilev's gravitational pull
was great, and certainly others stayed too long, until their own
atmospheres had been siphoned off and there was nothing sus-
tainable left. (Diaghilev's lover and star dancer Nijinsky had to
move to South America, marry a woman, and get himself in-
stitutionalized here in Switzerland to get away from the man.
It was no use, he had waited too many years and suffered too
much manipulation to get away entirely. His career was over.)
Switzerland must have offered a fateful break, a time to be one's
own self and not just a satellite.

They collaborated again in the future, but it was not the
same. Stravinsky approached Diaghilev as an equal; he was not
assigned work. He was not a student, not an employee, he was
a peer. And his work evolved more quickly, finding new forms
and new displays. And not all of his work went to Diaghilev anymore; he no longer owed him that.

* * *

There are problems with an American citizen with German residency trying to get a Russian travel visa while traveling in Switzerland, so I have to take the train to Geneva and straighten it out. My name, contorted from the Latin alphabet to Cyrillic and back again, has been rewritten, rendered down to Krispn.

"Can they do that?" I ask my lover.

"They probably assume you'll be needing a new identity if you're leaving for Russia. Maybe there was a box you were supposed to check on the application if not."

I will be leaving Switzerland soon, but I don't want to think about it. I have enjoyed my furlough. Done with my consulate duties, I walk to the museum of the Reformation. John Calvin, who believed that men and women were born with their fates predestined, and nothing they did in this lifetime could save them from hellfire if that is where God wanted them to be, was put in charge of Geneva and created a theocracy. It didn't go well, although it's hard to tell from the museum, which seems more focused on the furniture that everyone was using at the time than on the tumult.

Take away a person's sense of free will and see how they behave. Men murdered their wives in the street, believing if the impulse lived in them, they were headed for hellfire anyway. Those sure of their damnation went wild—why try for ascetic goodness if your soul will live in eternal torment no matter what? Clergy, intent on making a peaceful and orderly example of Geneva, ruled with a heavy hand, while stripping churches of ornamentation and religious art—it's all idolatry, it's all blasphemy. They destroyed people's imaginations, they seemed surprised the populace revolted.

I try to find the place where Michael Servetus was burned as a heretic during the reign of Calvin, but either I get turned around or it is not marked. Calvin was obsessed with who was with him and who was against him, and Servetus was decidedly against. He was one of those delicious polymaths who worked in everything from poetry to theology to philosophy to meteorology. He could translate the Bible from the original, and he knew both the Catholics and the Protestants were warping the text for their own advantages, and for this he was condemned to die.

He responded by traveling directly to Geneva. He stood in Calvin's church. He got in his face. I don't know if he was a willing martyr or if he thought Calvin would flinch. Whatever his motivations, he was set alight, like so many witches and heretics and outsiders before him.

I spend the night in the suburbs of Geneva in an acquaintance's medieval home, just on the other side of the French border. Paula and I are getting drunk on very nice Japanese whiskey, and the warmth starts in the belly and works its way out to the toes and then back up the legs, and as she tells me about the ghost who lives up in the corner of the room ("you should wave some burning sage up there," I tell her, "or find the body that must be buried in the walls and burn the bones, that is what they do on Supernatural"), I send ill-advised dirty e-mails to my lover.

"Then there was the time I lost my sense of smell."

That got my attention.

One day she fell on the ice, hitting her head, hard. She shook it off and didn't notice anything was wrong until she was cooking that night and thought all of her herbs must have dried out. She mentioned it off-handedly to her doctor, and then suddenly she was being sent into emergency brain surgery. The impact was so hard that it had severed the connection to the olfactory nerves. "I was in the hospital . . ."

"Wait, go back. Did your sense of smell come back?"

"Yes, but it's not the same." My friend writes about wines and spirits; she spent years, decades, refining her palate and learning the language of the aromas and the tastes. "It's strange. It's like I can't quite make the connection, I know that I know the smell but I can't name it."

I tell her my theory, that when we lose the thing we rely on most, our adaptations become our strengths. She looks at me like I am insane. I regain my conversational footing by telling her about the time I blew my ears out on an airplane and was deaf for a month. "It was kind of nice, not having to hear conversations in subways, walking around in silence." I tell her about Honeybee, who let me spend time making pasta in her kitchen, rolling out the dough and feeding it into the little hand-crank machine, not feeling the need to fill up the room with senseless chatter and gossip. We worked side by side in the quiet. "I almost miss it."

"Losing your sense of smell is terrible. I didn't want to eat, nothing tasted like anything. And now, writing is still a struggle."

She shows me to my room. I envy her beautiful house with her two enormous, sanguine cats. Her beautiful husband with the high-paying job. In the morning she'll set out a plate with an array of breads and jams, a soft-boiled egg, yogurt with various toppings, coffee to my exact specifications. It is a bounty I have not seen in months and it makes me want to cry. But for now I lie under the slanted roof, another first night in a foreign room, I forget where I even am, exactly. I was a little tipsy before I got into her car, then it was a blur of trees and border checkpoints and nice houses all in a row.

It's so comfortable, and I wonder what it is in me that chases discomfort. When my home life is stable, that is when I go to pieces. Perhaps the movement is necessary to keep myself from noticing that I'm always fraying, that bits of me are shredding off in the wind. Tomorrow I'll take the train back to the farmhouse, and I'll walk past the cows, who will think I am leading them somewhere—I will turn around and there will be a dozen beasts following me down the lane. I will make my own tea by boiling water in a saucepan, and I will carry my own groceries on my back. And then very soon I will pack up and do this again, somewhere else, configured slightly differently.

But I linger. With the pastry and the very good coffee and the conversation and the camaraderie. Maybe I'll return to Geneva one day and we will do this again. Most likely this is a fleeting moment that will not repeat itself, and I feel the ache in my chest as we sit together, missing it already. Missing Paula already, missing Switzerland. I know too that I will someday pad my life out again and I will miss the skeletal reduction. The pain is beautiful.

St. Petersburg /
W. Somerset Maugham

Girls in love, be harlots. It hurts less.

ELIZABETH SMART

I am languishing in Basel, waiting for the start date of my Russian visa, when a message comes in from the gentleman. "Come to France." It's been too long since I've had a conversation with someone I already know. Having to constantly sum up my existence for new acquaintances I am soon to abandon again anyway has been wearing me down and making me antisocial, or at least prone to fabrication. Particularly since no one would like the real answers to their questions about why I am out here traveling. "I am trying to find reasons to keep myself alive, and what is it that you do?"

I think about the last time the gentleman and I saw each other, in a Parisian apartment, with an entire bottle of whiskey and an ill-timed joke about what would happen if he knocked me up. Then, yelling and throwing things and sex that destroyed a couch. Sure, let's go, see what happens. I book my train ticket.

The first bottle of wine is opened within ten minutes of my arrival, and the rest of the evening hazes itself out. I wake up in the spare bedroom. Clothes off and only about halfway on the bed. He knocks and enters, carrying a full glass of red wine. "The world is terrible," I tell him, everything kind of lurching around in my head, in my stomach, in the room.

"I know," he responds. "This will help."

Over our days together I try to convince myself that this is romantic, the wine and the long walks around the city and the sex and the conversation under the stars. When I explain to my friends over e-mail where I am, in my telling it sounds like anything a woman could ever wish for. But the thought won't translate down into my body. When he touches me, I suddenly want to be on the other side of the room.

I leave early one morning, and he's asking me to come back in two weeks. I nod and assure him I will, but I know I won't. This experiment I've undertaken for the last eight years of being the woman with no needs has failed, and I make my way to the airport and then through security crying in a slow leak: every time I reach up to my face there is more to brush away.

But ending the experiment means returning to what came before, and what came before was many years of nothing. There was such an absence of love or even like for such a long time. Unrequited is my romantic template. And so when the only male attention on offer is sex, it's easier to convince yourself that is all you needed to begin with. That you are too busy and too independent for anything else, that romance is frivolous and you are serious. Rather than admit to yourself that the business and the independence and the seriousness was as much effect as cause, the result of a lot of years on your own.

So I leak all the way from airport to airport to airport, through multiple flights eastward and through a passport control line with no end and only stop when the terror of an 85-mph one-hand steering taxi ride into St. Petersburg distracts me for a minute. But if we are going to face down loneliness, Russia seems like the place to do it. And if we are going to face down the despair of the unloved, W. Somerset Maugham seems like the right guide.

* * *

By all accounts, W. Somerset Maugham's wife was a yeller and a thrower. A hysteric and a fury. By all accounts, she trapped him into a marriage by publicly using his name in her divorce. By all accounts, Syrie Maugham did not actually love her husband, unless it is possible to love someone without respecting their work, their interests, their needs, their emotional integrity. She wanted him to conform to her ideal of a husband, and that he didn't was his problem, not hers. And by all accounts, in the twelve years they were married, her husband spent as much time away from her as humanly possible, taking off with any excuse for a long journey in the company of the man he actually loved.

Things could have gone differently. Not with the man he loved—this was when homosexuality was still a crime, after all. But there were other routes available that were shut down, some by fate, some by Maugham, others by Syrie.

And had it all turned out differently, Maugham certainly would have been happier, but the rest of us might have suffered as a result.

* * *

W. Somerset Maugham is the bard of the toxic relationship. Starting in 1902 with *Mrs Craddock*, where a woman's life suddenly gets good as soon as her husband dies tragically, he examined in his novels the particular devastating effects an unmatched pair will have on one another. Certainly writers before him—Tolstoy, Henry James, whatever—have examined this subject, but no one else did it with such a gimlet eye, with such enthusiasm, or with such skepticism that this man-woman-in-a-home dynamic is the way society should be ordered.

In his books, men and women confuse sexual obsession with love, suffer disappointment, and then vow the other person's destruction; they scheme and they abuse and they choose badly and they prefer a fantasy over the real person standing in front of them. Mr. Craddock loves Mrs. Craddock, and he shows it by belittling her and denying her the pleasures and affections she so desperately needs. Philip in *Of Human Bondage* loves Mildred and nearly kills himself supporting her and wooing her and looking after her despite her lack of interest in him as a human being. *The Painted Veil*'s Walter loves Kitty, and so he drags her into the middle of a cholera epidemic in the hopes that one or both of them will die. In so many of his books, the death or removal of the spouse is the end to imprisonment.

So did he call Syrie to him? Before this incarnation, did he pledge himself to documenting the underbelly of love and passion, where everything is rot and slime, thus burdening himself with the worst possible match to help him along with the material? Of all the choices he could have made, a man into men (and a small smattering of women) and looking for a heterosexual cover, it seems like he could have found someone bland and wide in the middle, someone who could suffer silently through his disinterest because her hopes for love were not that high to begin with. Someone who was less of an embodiment of every relational nightmare he had been writing about, and would continue to write about until his death.

* * *

The same year that Maugham married Syrie, he was sent to St. Petersburg on a mission as a spy. It happened to be the year of the Russian Revolution as well. He had also spent time in France and Switzerland doing the same work, but of the Ashenden (the not-at-all-veiled spy/writer version of himself who serves as narrator) stories, the one I keep returning to is one set in St. Petersburg, "Mr. Harrington's Washing." Despite being sent by the British government on an impossible mission—to keep Russia from withdrawing from World War I—with no assets, no familiarity with the country, and no idea how to fulfill this plan, and despite being in a city that is obviously on the brink of revolution, his primary concern is with the woman he once loved dearly who is also in the city.

It seems realistic to me. I should be the type of writer who investigates the darkening of sexual freedom in Russia, as Putin's government throws gay activists in jail, threatens gay tourists with deportation, and outlaws the word *gay*. I should be investigating corruption and cronyism. I should find a way to sneak into the prison where Pussy Riot members are being held and conduct an exclusive interview. Instead I am lying in bed a lot, eating smoked fish on black bread, and waiting for the e-mail from my lover that tells me he has moved out and left his wife. We can say this lethargy is connected to the horrible pattern of the bodies of Russian journalists discovered with bullets in their brains, but it's a thin cover.

But then calling Maugham a spy is overselling it a little. He served his country and all its covert operations, but he carried no poison-tipped umbrella. He reported that being a spy was mostly a drudgery and a bore. Waiting around for messages, decoding the messages, recoding new messages, playing bridge in a hotel while his new message is being delivered. In "Washing," Ashenden does his part to keep Russia in the war seemingly by taking a lot of lunches, and no one in power cares that his mission fails and the entire nation falls apart. Someone should have sent me out here with a decoder ring. If one can save the world through waiting for people to write and checking for new messages, I could have solved any number of international crises by now.

There's no hint of Syrie in the Ashenden stories, as autobiographical as everyone says they are. By the time he was traveling through Europe as a spy, his fate with her was sealed. And yet there are no stories about impending doom or walls slowly closing in, even if he must have known that was what was happening. His daughter by Syrie had already been born, and his name was used in the papers when discussing her divorce from the pharmaceutical millionaire Henry Wellcome. He was going to have to marry her if he did not want to be ostracized from society. Or revealed as a queer. He had come of age during Oscar Wilde's trial; he was all too aware that being labeled a sodomite could be a death sentence. He was going to have to marry this woman, and so undertaking dangerous missions in war zones, I guess, looked like a good delaying tactic. Or perhaps Syrie is in these stories, disguised as the war itself.

But this was a common topic of their arguments, that she did not inspire him. She was not his muse. His retort was that she had no inner world, no depths. Shallow socialites do not inspire great works of literature. And maybe Syrie did not show up in the books, but the marital rage and the sense of marriage as a disease-carrier came out in almost everything he wrote after her.

* * *

So I am trying to find Maugham in a city that hosted him only briefly. His ghost resides elsewhere. Any remains he left behind—fingerprints, a forgotten pair of cufflinks, an overfull ashtray with half his personal brand and the other half smeared with red lipstick—have been washed away. But maybe it's not his ghost I'm after, it's the ghost of their marriage. And that seems like it would reside in the all-too-often-smeared-with-blood streets of St. Petersburg all right.

Otherwise I'm not sure what to make of this city. I am an off-scale doll shoved into a mismatched dollhouse in the back of a secondhand store. The scale of the city is enormous. The palaces were built to replicate French architecture but are stretched wider and higher, and the effect for the foreigner is to feel as if maybe oneself has shrunk, rather than that the buildings are a bit too big. The squares look as if they were built specifically to house an angry mob, and the streets are wide enough that only a tank would look natural coasting down them. Even the churning, dark river, more inlet than river really, gushing endlessly into the sea, is too aggressive. And yet people, they just stomp over it carrying bags of groceries or walking their dogs, rather than tiptoeing over the bridges or throwing in offerings, which seems like the more reasonable response.

The first residents had to be bribed to live here. Rather than organically grown from shifting populations, nomadic wanderers finally deciding *here*, the city was built, placed on the earth by the decision of one man. As a result, the foundations of the city aren't in the land, they are in Peter the Great's psyche. He didn't much care about the needs of his people his people would do what he told them to do. And so at the Arctic border he built palaces and residences that were more appropriate for the warmer climate of France, and he scaled the thing to an emperor's ego rather than a human body. He meant the city to be a symbol, and it is, but it is a symbol of the separation between the reality of the ruler and the daily life of the people, rather than of Russia's great spirit.

Peter the Great lingers in his city. From his enthusiastic participation in the interrogation torture of criminals and traitors to his cultured and sophisticated mind to his great love of female company, all of that exists in the form of the long shadows of the towering monuments and the opera houses and the brightly colored palaces, all surfaces gilding and shining. But the gold and the jewels and the ornate decorations start to feel sarcastic after a while.

St. Petersburg exists because one man said, why not. And he built it not because the city was shimmering from another dimension in all its potentiality. He won some land in a battle, and he wanted to make sure he could keep it. It was built on land that was a swamp in the summer and an icy hellscape in the winter, and he built it to mark territory.

Even the subway stinks of the uncanny, a long descent into the underworld. Situated much farther underground than in most cities, it has escalators that are endless. If you don't know what you're getting into, the first trip is disconcerting. From the top you cannot see the bottom. And your ears pop and you can't turn around to go back up. Minutes pass, you are still on your way down. This is normal, people are responding as if this is normal, so stop looking back up in the hopes of a glimmer of daylight still visible, it's not. No beginning visible, no ending visible, just a slow-moving purgatory. But finally people are straightening themselves up from that hopeless butt-slump against the railing, we must be nearing the end.

And then, at the bottom: a billboard-sized illuminated picture of a kitten. All orange fuzz and tilted head. I wasn't sure I wasn't imagining it, maybe I had suffered some kind of hallucination on the long way down. But no, it's really there. It's not advertising anything, there's nothing written on the photo at all. Just an apology, maybe, from the makers of the demonic escalator.

I am entranced by St. Petersburg, but I am exhausted by it. I keep getting lost in the wooded park between the subway and my apartment. I get distracted by the people, the balloons, the bakery carts, the noise and hum of it, and suddenly I am in a whole other part of the city and I have no idea how to get home.

A friend who knows Russia well e-mails to ask how it is going.

"I am spending a lot of time in bed."

"Yes. It's like not jet lag when you go there, it's existential lag. Naps are important."

* * *

The world presented an alternative to Syrie. Pre-Syrie. Before Maugham maybe even knew Syrie existed. He fell for a woman. Not just any woman, a slut. A vivacious, flirty, slutty little woman who tantalized him with her wit and her gaiety. He loved her. He was always so trapped in himself, so shy and restricted, and here was a woman who had none of those issues and yet still had a refined mind and a cultured interest in the arts. And she knew he was gay, and not in a "deep down I knew there was something . . . different" kind of way, she just knew. And they had a laughing little affair, and maybe stayed up hitting the brandy and swapping stories about men conquered, who knows. She went off to the States to act in a play, and Maugham came up with a vision of how life could be.

Here is how life could be: A man and a woman could coexist in one house as equals. They could love each other and be affectionate with one another, and still not jealously lay claim to one another. He could fuck the pool boy. She could fuck the pool boy. They could have separate but coexisting lives, and then come together at cocktail hour to tell stories and play cards.

We all start out like this in our relationships—this particular match-up, this is going to be the one that does not end in her setting fire to his belongings in the driveway or him running off with a twenty-six-year-old with a lower-back tattoo—and hopefully the fall between the ideal and the reality doesn't break our necks. Who knows how far that fall would have been with Maugham and his delightful little slut. It never got a chance to be.

Maugham asked for her hand in marriage. Unbeknownst to him, the slut had just discovered she was pregnant and had agreed to marry the man who had done the deed. Who knows what this other man's pitch was. You will be my wife and this child's mother, and then you won't be ostracized or called a whore. Maugham laid out his vision for her, but maybe in her state she could not work up the idealism. If perhaps he had shown up only a few days earlier, before she knew what was growing inside her, she could still have answered with youthful courage. She might not have had any trouble shaking convention in her single life on the stage, but now she would have to do it with the full weight of illegitimate pregnancy, another twenty or so years of fertility, and society's expectations for the conduct of women pressing down on her. She must have known there was nowhere they could set up their house that would be far enough away from the scolds and the gossips, who would be all too happy to spread scandal and ruin careers.

The little slut said no. (The gods said no.) She married her man, became respectable. She died soon after, unhappy. And Maugham was left alone to collide into Syrie.

* * *

Now that all of the intellectuals are atheists, you hear this reasoning an awful lot: If there is a God, and he is all-powerful, why is there evil? Why are there genocide and children with bone cancer and typhoons that destroy everything in their path? Surely if there were a God, there would be no suffering.

Which seems like the kind of theological argument that would come out of the mouth of a seven-year-old who was just denied a candy bar. Why bother having any creation at all if it was not imperfect and fucked up? What would be the point of a little sphere of perfection? The perfection would just blip itself out. Perfection cannot hold. And that gap, between reality and the ideal, will always present itself to us as suffering.

I don't believe that God only gives you as much as you can

handle, I've known too many murderers and suicides for that, people who one day just couldn't find their way back. To me the suffering isn't the point, it is the method. The way it shakes us, breaks us wide open, forcing us in contact with one another. The point is what you do then.

The part of me who is a compassionate human being wishes Maugham had a life of love and peace and happiness, of unconditional support and tenderness. Someone to pour him a drink and laugh at his jokes and listen to his stories. Someone who would wish him good-bye when he left on his travels and didn't mind who the companion was. And someone who would have his or her jokes laughed at, drinks poured, wished good-bye when he or she left on personal adventures. This part of me would like to rewrite his biography with wishful thinking and then have it be true.

The part of me who is miserable and lonely and always laying herself down next to predators appreciates the company and the wise insight of his novels. The part of me who is pure spinster is grateful for Maugham's spinsters, who are always carting off somewhere exciting, in control of their own finances, making out with sailors.

And that part of me knows that wisdom is hard won. And that wisdom is another thing that suffering is for.

* * *

Peter the Great wanted to introduce Russia to Europe, but he found Russia so embarrassing, like a social climber mortified by her Appalachian kin. The Russians were superstitious and xenophobic, and god, the weird shit they wear. He could never invite European dignitaries, coming from their sphere of Enlightenment and science and witty conversation, to his backward country.

Peter's solution: dictate a change in dress. If you were in

his company, you had to abandon the Russian robes and hats and jewelry, and you had to present yourself clean-shaven. Approach bearded and Peter took out a knife and hacked off your whiskers himself. You had to dress like a European, with the stockings and the heeled boots and the tailored jackets.

Come winter, however, the Russian as European did not fare so well. His hands no longer covered by the ballooning sleeves, his torso left unprotected by the thick layers, his shins and face exposed to the Arctic air. Frostbite and exposure followed. The Russian had to choose whether to be respectable, whether all of this was worth risking death. But then again, being outside of the czar's graces never led to much of a lifespan either.

* * *

We agree to these things socially and culturally, just because everyone else has done it, just because it would be embarrassing to explain our variation. And then, once we've shaped ourselves unnaturally and adjusted to the discomfort, we insist to others they do the same. We tell them it's unhealthy to be walking around any other way. We tell them it has to be and has never been any different.

So the rules of relationships seem to me. (So says the spinster.) Where infidelity is a deal breaker and anything other than monogamy is seen as madness, where cohabitation is mandatory, where "healthy" is prioritized over passionate, or inspirational, or exciting.

The only god that the other gods and goddesses were terrified of was Eros. With one arrow he could ruin their lives entirely. Suddenly they are passionately in love with a tree or a mortal, or a cow maybe. Someone completely wrong for them. Because love is not cozy nights on a couch. It is getting hit by a bus. It is being dragged into deep water with no objects of buoyancy. The gods knew that. We humans, always needing things to be tidy and understandable and rational and comfortable, are willing to lop off the most interesting parts of love just to make it fit.

I have become obsessed with reading advice columns, particularly one woman who writes for a well-regarded website and answers every relationship question with the same formula: insisting the querent leave their "dysfunctional" relationship, get extensive therapy, and then listen to the columnist crow about her heteronormative marriage that consists of emotional stability and a weekly date night. That is the goal, she cries, that is the reward you get after the mountain of self-help and therapeutic exploration. I project all of my fears of dead passion and moribund relationships onto her marriage, this person I have never met. I want to say to her, Your relationship, where he's just there, all of the time, every night in your bed. Where you eat together and have couple friends you meet for dinner. Your relationship, where you have to schedule sex to make sure you have it, where your week rotates around what's on the television. A house where you have to subsume, and sacrifice, and negate most of your desires because they would hurt the feelings of this other person who is subsuming, sacrificing, and negating most of his own. A marriage where you schedule one vacation a year, to some beach in an impoverished country, and you aren't allowed to just fuck off on your own, where you alternate whose family you visit at the holidays. Those things, right there, that looks like madness to me. And it feels like death.

In my head she tells me that is an immature way to look at relationships. Unrealistic. "You are only staying with him because you're scared of real love, and real vulnerability."

I'm scared of something. But it's not real love. I am projecting, that much is clear. I am trying to justify my own misery so that I don't have to do anything about it. But it is also clear to me that quiet domesticity would take me out faster than this tormented affair.

* * *

All this talk about what is natural and what is unnatural between a man and a woman and in the makeup of a family, as if we could know. As if we are not born of culture and shaped by culture, as if it would ever be possible to correctly interpret the ghostly messages of our prehistorical DNA, and as if what we could learn there would ever make us happy.

If there ever were one moment where everything worked for us, where we lived in harmony and at ease with our natures, then we would still be there. There is no garden to return to, no idyllic perfect childhood, no enwombed state. The Garden of Eden was boring, childhood is a nightmare we should all be grateful to be done with, and your mother smoked while she was pregnant and poisoned you in the womb with artificial sugar substitutes. The best thing any of us can do is to just keep fucking up in a forward motion, and see what comes out of it.

* * *

There is something strange, that never goes away, about these boom cities. There are cities that have fixed themselves into the earth, that exist within their own history and seem as if they will always be there. St. Petersburg is not one of these cities. Moscow is. It is not simply Moscow's medieval history, it is all that came before it. It is all of the bones of the inhabitants and passers-through, the Slavs and the raiders and the raided who fled, all who laid claim here. The city feels natural, as natural as a city can feel. People throughout time have wandered here and chosen to stay, from huts to stone to brick to steel. The roots go a long way down.

I am not saying St. Petersburg is not grand. It is grand. But it has the sense of a city of frosting. One good downpour and it'll all wash away.

Placed via whim or for defense, you can feel it under your feet, its ability and maybe inclination to uproot itself and skitter elsewhere. In the morning, as I walk from my little suburb into the city proper, there is always the sense that perhaps today it won't be there. Maybe it will have shifted east, and then how will I ever find my favorite bakery again? If it decides to throw itself into the sea, will I be thrown too? Or will I and all of the other inhabitants be left behind, waking on the cold ground.

* * *

I think about what Syrie was getting out of this marriage, because obviously she was getting something. Otherwise get a divorce, get a financial settlement, get a house you don't have to pay for, go see the world and send the ex-husband the bill. That is the way it worked in those days, and she married a fortune and divorced with a fortune. A divorcée has more financial and sexual freedom than a spinster, so this was not about respectability. If your primary act as a wife is the slow destruction of your beloved, why not try to take up knitting and see if that is just as fun?

It's not coincidental that she didn't need another marriage and another husband to torment (she was wildly and publicly unfaithful to her first husband) once she built herself a career. She became an interior decorator and finally found something else to amuse her. Which was filling rooms with white furnishings and white carpets and painting walls white, and okay, I guess that qualifies as contributing to humanity.

I understand my tone is bitter. I have seen men in my life laid low by these types of women. I have also lived with their male counterparts, who bullied and threatened, who tormented and humiliated. Who woke me up at 4 a.m. with a drunken leer and a "You know what your problem is?" I know all of the elaborate ways we take apart the people we love, and all the ways we allow ourselves to be taken apart. And I know that the most powerful abuse does not come in the form of a blow to the face.

* * *

> I did everything I could for you and when I couldn't do what you wanted I do not feel I deserved the hard and cruel things you said to me. You want my affection and I have given it to you—you do not know how much—but you seem to have done all you could to kill it. Do you know that no one in all my life has said the things you have said to me? No one has ever complained of me and nagged me and harassed me as you have. How can you expect me to preserve my affection for you? You have terrorized me.
>
> W. SOMERSET MAUGHAM, regarding his wife Syrie, in his memoir *Looking Back*

* * *

As with every bad marriage, all the people in their life had an opinion on how it went wrong, whose fault it was. Anecdotes and innuendos came out in gossip columns, friends took sides in the breakup. When Maugham aired his complaints against his ex-wife in *Looking Back*, that she needed constant attention and was vindictive and abusive, as well as making public her multiple affairs, friends lined up to say Syrie always seemed like grace and warmth itself at dinner parties, as if nasty things with gills and sharp teeth don't lie just beneath the surface of plenty of marriages. After Maugham died one of Syrie's friends published a vile little book called *A Case of Human Bondage* which stops just short of calling him a queer but explicitly calls him a tyrant. But then its author, Beverley Nichols, was once one of Maugham's lovers as well, tossed aside.

But Nichols tells of an evening, way after Maugham had given up on his marriage. Way after the haranguing and her desperate neediness. Way after Maugham simply refused even to set foot back in England, he needed so much space from her. Syrie decided to fight to win him back. If he refused to go to England, she would go to the south of France. And buy a villa next to his. And redecorate it. And then force an encounter by inviting over all of his society friends to witness how reasonable and devoted she was being and how unhinged he was. Still, she was surprised he chose not to be with her.

We are awfully beholden to this idea that only men are abusers. That if a marriage is bad, the man must be the victimizer and the woman the victim. Because while many of Maugham's biographers, particularly Selina Hastings, try valiantly to understand Syrie's motivations and make her sympathetic, if the genders were reversed and Syrie became the husband, s/he would be despised as a bully and a stalker.

To anyone who has ever been on the receiving end of Syrie's type of affection, her actions are entirely familiar. Her needs and wants are so great that no one else's can even be considered. If she cannot be loved, as no amount of love can fill such an abyss, she will nourish herself on blood.

This is something Maugham's books know deeply: the interaction of black hole and star. The way sometimes we pull to us the person who knows exactly how to undo us. It was his romantic template.

* * *

I cannot sleep. I thought the white nights of St. Petersburg's summer would be romantic, but instead they cause my intermittent insomnia to become chronic. My body thinks when we lie down with the sky still lit up that surely we are just going to nap, and I awake after forty minutes. When it's not the sun, it is the swarm of mosquitoes in my room, which dart away out of sight the second the light goes on, and dive directly at my head when it goes off.

As I Google Image search for pictures of Maugham's French villa, the Villa Mauresque, a gossip rag's article about the reality show *The Bachelor* shows up in the search results. Surely not, I think, but yes, a season of the UK's version of *The Bachelor* used Maugham's home, now converted into a boutique hotel, as the romantic backdrop.

I download the season—illegally, because there is no way I am giving those people my money—and watch it late at night, the laptop pulled close to my chest. This villa hosted Maugham at his most "oh fuck it." It was where he could openly associate with his male lovers, where said lovers and associates could walk around his estate naked, where drinks and drugs and sex could be had without shame or hiding.

And now this is where the Bachelor, with his flashy watch and professionally whitened teeth, can cavort with trashy Barbie girls, so tricked out with blond hair extensions and false eyelashes and surgically altered breasts and spray tans that it is difficult to tell one from another. Where Maugham found his middle-aged freedom after a decade of living with Syrie, a twenty-three-year-old man with the world at his feet announces he is ready to settle down with "the one."

After I watched the whole season and had come to feel like maybe I could use a trepanation or something to let out the evil spirits that had invaded my body through the ears and eyes, the Internet tells me that this was the last season of *The Bachelor*. Undying love was declared, and then once the cameras were off the couple never saw each other again. She started a relationship with someone else, and he got back together with an ex, and the only intimacy they shared was a series of barbs directed at one another through the tabloids.

I see the work of Maugham's angry ghost in th_s develop-
ment, furious that this harmless bunny version of love—all
champagne and roses, hot tubs and soft-focus frenching, talk
of lifelong devotion and destiny—is still poisoning the masses.
I can feel his smirk from the other side.

* * *

Terrified of the subway, I walk around and across St. Petersburg. I walk despite the enormity of the city and the hours it
takes to get anywhere. I walk to shut out unhelpful thought
processes, and then I walk until I'm so tired the thoughts meet
no resistance and crowd in noisily. I walk again and again to the
State Russian Museum to stand in front of the Mikhail Vrubel
paintings of dark visions and unstoppable forces. I walk until
my little gold flats have holes in the bottom and I can feel the
pavement with the soles of my feet. I buy cigarettes and think
about taking up smoking. I don't talk to anyone.

I get lost a lot, mistaking one canal for another and then
off I go until I almost reach Finland. My own neighborhood is
mostly Soviet modernism, these heavy blocks that add up to
a strange, stark beauty. Many lie abandoned, one looks like a
regular apartment building except for the few trees growing
out of the top windows and dilapidated roof. It shifts, once you
cross the river, to the European style with the wide gardens and
gold spackled onto every surface. Only occasionally does something wild and Russian present itself, all squiggles and zigzags,
seemingly designed by a child who believes that the drawing
that uses the most crayons out of the box is the most beautiful.
It must have been this that Peter tried so hard to keep out of
his city, but the buildings sprang up through the Church, also a
constant source of embarrassment for the leader.

But when the Parisian and Viennese mathematicians were
working with the idea of infinity, they started being sent away

to asylums and dying by their own hand as a result, unable to stretch their rational, linear skulls around the idea. It was the Russian mystics, with their embarrassing beards and wearing all the wrong outfits, who were excited and not terrified, who were able to take infinity and set theory further. Their worlds had never been finite to begin with.

* * *

Is it appropriate to ask a writer to suffer on our behalf? It is good that both parties are dead, yes? And that all we are left with are the wonderful books that came out of the abuse.

(But then of course Maugham and Syrie had a daughter, and that daughter had children, and so on. And we all know that misery won't just stay in one place, it has an awful tendency to seep downward. All those nights of yelling and cursing and weeping, they must have echoes.)

* * *

There is something I'm trying to pull out of all of this. If there's one thing that reading Maugham's books and Maugham's life has taught me, it is that we don't all get to have a love that makes sense to us. Maugham had his gentleman, and they had some good times together, but then he watched that man become a drunk and a gambler, and then he watched that man die.

When my friends tell me I deserve someone wonderful, my future true love is surely out there somewhere, I can feel myself hardening and the countermeasures kick in. Don't listen to them, don't let your hope get out of control. The fall between the ideal and the reality does break my neck. I'm still alone here, in this enormous bed and my fog of malarial mosquitoes, in a city where my lover was supposed to meet me but then couldn't because of the wife, and now my neck can't even crane upward anymore. I have to keep my head down, to plow through another insomniac night halfway around the world from anyone who knows me and to try to keep that despair from ruining what the world has to offer me. And the world has so much to offer. Even just here, within this one city block, I have a grocery store with a salad display case a million miles long. Every day I select two new salads to eat with my smoked fish and black bread, and still I have not worked my way through half of the offerings. I have a fruit stand in the other direction, where I can buy a pound of the most wonderful cherries for I have no idea how much money, I haven't really worked out the currency or exchange rates yet. And the sublet I found comes with a piano I can only play "Old King Wenceslas" on and a pair of very spindly heels in my size that I can wear to tart around the apartment. I can know how wonderful it is to be here as long as I can wall up a very specific part of my brain.

But the words said in kindness and love, by people who have romantic histories that consist of something other than brambles and thorn bushes, terrorize me. And I don't know if staying with this man is an act of pessimism or optimism.

I can't read love stories with happy endings, that black hole of self-pity in my chest opens up and threatens to swallow me. I need the acid of W. Somerset Maugham to remind me, people survive their loneliness. It happens. And great joy can come even if there's no one else there to share it.

So I spend my birthday in proper spinster fashion, with a night at the Russian ballet, wearing a ridiculous dress and sparkly shoes, sipping champagne and eating little caviar sandwiches, smoking on the rooftop without inhaling, just kind of lighting the cigarettes and waving them around, and looking out to the river that flows to the Baltic. I would wear a little fur shrug if it weren't a million degrees outside. I taxi my way home, the driver says, "Oh, you're American!" and turns on Bon Jovi loudly. I had this album on cassette tape in my white trash youth. He rocks out and I glide through the city charioted. I fall asleep in the not-darkness and manage to stay asleep until morning.

*   *   *

Late in his career, Maugham presented the character of Rosie in *Cakes and Ale*. She was a lively and warm woman, who initiated the narrator not only into sex but also into affection. Because sex with her was not possession. There was no way to stake a claim on her territory, she was her own person. And she enjoyed the company of many men, but that did not diminish the connection she had with any of them.

Rosie is, in fact, the only positive portrayal of a slut I have ever read in literature. She does not come to a bad end, there is no throwing of the self under the train or walking into the sea. And she does not reveal a heartbreaking tale of abandonment and want from her childhood to explain why she has no interest in a committed marriage, nothing to explain why she cannot give or receive love. Rosie gives and receives love. To and from multiple suitors. And she dies a magnificent old lady who lived a life of exactly her own choosing.

Maugham rewrote the story of his little slut to give her the life in print he could not give her in the world. But not even in the fictional world can he live a life by her side; that life eludes him even in his imagination.

*   *   *

I am back to reading *A Case of Human Bondage*, alternating it with Maugham's (bitter) account of his marriage *Looking Back*, written after his wife's death, and a thought emerges: I must kill every man I have slept with. Or at least outlive them, to keep some catty account of my weaker moments from making its way into print. It is an embarrassing string of men. Some writers, some poets, one bookseller. Some, you know, guys who were at the bar.

And now I just kind of wish them all dead. The gentleman included. Most of all him. He is the last remnant, the last lingering thread to that past, and now he stands in for all of them. Those slutty years that mostly weren't even fun. It was just that I couldn't go one more day without being touched, and paying for another massage to fill that need was just too humiliating. I took what I could get.

I have two spare weeks, this two-week hole in my schedule, and the gentleman is e-mailing again, he would like me to return to France. I do not delude myself that it is the pleasure of my company he longs for. I am an easy lay and I don't ask questions about where he has been. I take a slug of whatever this Russian herbal liqueur is, that tastes like all the creatures of the forest got together to gift the world this pine needle dark earth decomposed leaf sludge squirrel tail mushroom and tree bark concoction, it is delicious. And I book two weeks in Budapest instead. Because I think better of myself. Despite all evidence to the contrary.

Reading Maugham's life, right up to the point in St. Petersburg, as the city erupts around him and he hastily makes an exit, it feels like the moment in a horror movie when the idiot girl goes back into the house. I grab the arms of my chair, I feel the air leave my body, and I swallow my scream, "Don't go back there!" Maybe staying in apocalyptic Russia, with his strange Russian ex-lover (a woman in the story, but who knows in real life), would have been less dangerous than going back into the house with the psycho with the ax standing behind the door.

He didn't really make it out of the house intact. Maugham never recovered from Syrie or any of his other disappointments in love. In his later life, he was always described as bitter and reptilian. A lifetime of forcing your head down, managing your expectations, that takes its toll.

The new e-mail sound swooshes on my phone. He's left his wife. He wants to see me. I don't know what to do.

London / Jean Rhys

> So they have courses teaching you foreign languages and
> ballroom dancing and etiquette and cooking. But there are
> no classes to learn how to be by yourself in a furnished room
> with chipped dishes, or how to be alone in general without any
> words of concern or familiar sounds.
>
> IRMGARD KEUN

The first thing I notice is I can understand the conversations
going on around me. We've switched to English somewhere
between Budapest and London, and I can feel the relief down
to my toes. No more rehearsing words and sentences and pro-
nunciation compulsively in my head as I approach the grocery
store, readying myself for the complicated task of ordering
one kilo of pork shoulder at the butcher counter. And that's in
countries where I know a few words; in places like Russia and
Budapest it was mostly pointing, miming, an elaborate game
of charades that occasionally veered into the obscene when I
discovered that in some places tampons are stashed behind the
counter.

But by the time the plane lands, and one train takes me to another train and then to another train, I am fed up with the English language. In the forty minutes from Luton to King's Cross
I was the unwilling spectator to the most awkward of conversations, awkward and yet incredibly loud for an enclosed space. A
man, seemingly just out of jail or some sort of institution, meet-

ing his parents, who are taking him home. And the parents tenderly, haltingly, trying to avoid the obvious questions: Who the fuck are you and didn't we give you enough love? enough attention? What else could you possibly want from us, do you even see what you are doing to your mother? And so the young man makes jokes about the food "in there," and the father squirms and crosses his arms, and the mother stares at the floor, and then loud proclamations about the weather are made.

Oh, take me back to Budapest, where I would not be invited into everyone's vulnerabilities, let me go back where I am perpetually misunderstood.

I struggle with my bag through King's Cross, putting serious consideration into just leaving it here in the subway tunnel and letting the antiterrorism unit blow it up as a suspected bomb, and I will just go out into the world with what I'm wearing right now forever and ever, this goddamn fucking thing.

The sublet I have rented is in a not very good neighborhood, and there are no forks for some reason, and the Craigslist girl I am subletting it from is an insane person, and the whole building shakes as the traffic outside races by. But I could afford it. Kind of. And I am in a city with English-language bookstores, no more selecting from the only two books that are not Harry Potter or Ken Follett occupying one sad shelf at the very back of a Russian shop. And there are people here who know me, and I will always (probably, I hope) understand what it is I am buying at the grocery store, how exciting. I get so happy to be in London that I instantly burn myself out, going from exhilaration to "oh shit, where is the bed" in about ten minutes. By 7 p.m. I am lying on a towel on a bare mattress, since there are no clean sheets, feeling the city rumble around me, anticipating tomorrow and all that the city might bring me.

* * *

There is something allegorical going on when I am in London, some sort of interaction between major city and small-town girl: suddenly I start humming all of those ballads of girls lost in the newly industrial age, girls who wandered off from the safety of their father's home to earn a wage, girls who should have stayed on the farm. ("Oh poor Liza poor girl, oh poor Liza Jane . . .") All those poor girls who died in factory fires, all those poor girls who turned to selling their bodies to be able to afford to heat their rooms, all those poor girls swallowed up by the uncaring city. ("And if a trick don't turn on me, I'll live until I die. Oh poor Liza poor girl . . .")

And we keep coming, we small-town girls, to the city that offers more adventure, more opportunity, more sex and excitement and money and glamour than the dusty little towns we came from. And some of us, we fall through the cracks. Some of us, we become offerings to the gods of the city, sacrificed on the altars of capitalism and ambition. There's something about it that shakes me to my core.

I was in London at nineteen, totally terrified, certain I would be obliterated somehow, sold off to the pirates or put to work in a coal mine. I hadn't really read much contemporary London literature, I was a century or so behind. The city kept trying to offer me kindnesses, like a store named Crispin's that I stumbled upon—I do not often see my name out in the wild like that—and a drunken night walking home from the bar in the moonlight, singing Tom Waits songs with a quite lovely man who was not interested in me "in that way." And then at twenty-seven I returned, and I found myself in a gallery standing before two Claude Cahun photographs, just by coincidence. But still, I was scared. Scared to take the subway, scared to venture too far on my own.

But then I had read so many of those *Sister Carrie* books, so many of those detective novels, all of those girls lost in the city /

decaying foundations of decency novels, that the narrative had slipped deep into my unconscious. The big shapeless form of London was trying to make friends, and I would run shrieking away, ahhhh it's a monster run for your lives! I had forgotten that the women in these novels were never women, they were always stand-ins for innocence and purity and morality. Their downfall was the downfall of society, not of an individual.

Maybe that was why I started to read Jean Rhys. Her women were being ground down in London and Paris, but at least they were women. They were not marble sculptures, bosoms exposed and representing some virtuous ideal. Men still write women as allegorical innocence, representations of the loss of innocence and the rise of violence. Read any murder mystery clogging shelves and brain pathways like artery plaque. She was pure, she was beautiful, that was why she had to die, so that the world-weary detective could pontificate on the state of society.

The city does take some of us down, but it's not happening to allegories, it's happening to people. And Jean Rhys's women—damage walking—see the worst of it, the city at its most merciless. Her books are about the moment you wake at 3 am. and realize you cannot go back to sleep, and all of the fears that come out to play at that hour and how very long it is until dawn. Her books are about being poor and hungry and having no one to turn to. Her books are about how nice it is, really, to just sit here and stop trying, to let the world go on without you as you fill your glass with melancholy and booze. They are about giving up and losing strength and never having anyone come to your aid. And the prose, the prose is so beautiful and stark. There is nothing metaphorical about it, it is plain and strong and bold. Beautiful books of misery, but without the Lost Innocence aftertaste.

I knew two things coming into this city: I hated London, and I loved Jean Rhys novels. Those were my certainties.

* * *

Between the wars, at the time of Jean Rhys, there was fuss and fluster about the New Woman. The New Woman was independent and probably had a secretarial job. She went on dates, maybe even had sex—oooh! It was the empowered version of the lost girl, the same initial trajectory (small town to big city), but instead of ending up dead or poor, she married the boss and restarted the Good Woman story, with the kids and the suburbs and quiet domesticity.

That is what the heroines of Jean Rhys novels were supposed to do but maybe could not. Too sensitive, too unlucky. They were all so very far from home, but the better life kept slipping from their delicate fingers. The New Woman life was revealed as empty and simply the same fur-lined trap that had foiled previous generations of women, but Rhys's women lacked the steely resolve required to cut through and find a third way.

And Jean Rhys was no New Woman herself, that was a role for girls with more confidence and more savvy. Rhys was a girl from the British West Indies, a girl with a not very loving or nurturing family. Smart girls from bad families don't look at another domestic scene as being their sanctuary. But the rest of Jean Rhys's life was elusive to me, I would need to learn more. I knew she was Ford Madox Ford's mistress for a while and that they later traded shitty versions of each other in their novels. But that seems typical for writers. I was going to have to do some digging, even though I knew that sometimes knowing too much about a writer can kill off one's affection for their work.

* * *

About seven years ago, there was a strange news item that people couldn't stop passing around. A thirty-eight-year-old woman in London had lain dead for three years in her apartment before her body was discovered. Joyce Vincent was found, her television still on, reduced to almost skeletal remains, and no one had reported her missing. She had friends, ex-boyfriends, four sisters. At the time of her death, her father was still alive. No one wondered where she was. Or so the story that circulates goes.

She was one of those girls who come to the city looking for a better life. She made herself entirely new. She cut off her family, dropped old friends. When she picked up a new boyfriend, she took on his life as her own, adopting his social circle and his aspirations. But no one has come forward who really knows what happened in the last two years of her life, how she went from a well-paid employee of a finance company to working as a cleaner, from living in her own flat in a nice neighborhood to living in a subsidized bedsit for battered women. No one seems to know who the man was who drove her there.

An ad for a documentary about Vincent asks, "If you died, how long would it take for someone to find you?" and that question calls to the Lonely Girl in each of us, it sings us songs about being unsafe, it tells us that deep down we are unloved and the city cares not a whit. Its chorus rings, Find Someone, Find Someone, Find Someone. Someone at least to file a missing person's report or identify your body. Blog posts and hysterical news articles say the fabric of our lives is fraying, that we can all end up like this poor woman. We are so disconnected, with our smartphones and our virtual friendships, on the wild tundra of the urban environment, all in danger of being lost forever. Slipping into nothingness. And just like that, another dead woman becomes allegory.

* * *

Jean Rhys is the feminine Ernest Hemingway. They were less than ten years apart in age. My comparison has a little to do with how they documented this lost generation of wandering expats and their mutually mercilessly reduced prose, but mostly I mean that in the way they were trapped in their specific gender display. Hemingway in his *I will simply open this blocked door by slamming my head into it repeatedly why not* masculinity, Rhys in her *can you please carry my bag and my other bag and my entire life I just can't* femininity. That display clouds the work of both writers, because while both are tremendously gifted, they seem unaware of that final limitation in their writing, that moment when gender becomes pathology. Even their careers were shaped by their ideas of how they should behave as their sex. Hemingway with his ambitious need for applause became the voice of his generation because he insisted that he become so. Rhys, who would have seen reaching for a goal as crass, simply wrote little novels and waited for someone to notice. She even waited for permission from the various men in her life to begin writing.

Here in London I have English-language bookstores. I buy a biography of Jean Rhys. I sit on my subletted couch in a neighborhood that was just a while back run through with rioting malcontents, smashing and burning and looting everything. Jean is growing up in a paradisiacal Dominica, having her first experiences of being interfered with by men, living her rather privileged colonial upbringing, with appropriately distant and rigid colonial parents. Once her biography gets her to London, though, I start to think, *Oh, did I read this same biography once long ago and forget?* This is awfully familiar, and I can predict what happens next.

But then I realize no, it was *Voyage in the Dark* I was thinking of. Anna/Jean is a chorus girl. Anna/Jean is living in a depressing little bedsit, until she meets her man with money. Anna/Jean falls in love with this person, seemingly just because he buys her things, he does not in particular seem to have any qualities.

Anna/Jean falls pregnant. Anna/Jean's abortion is paid for by this man, and he continues to support her even after he breaks up with her.

The biography gets her to Paris. Sasha/Jean is having trouble with her marriage. Sasha/Jean drinks more than she eats. Julia/Jean has always been supported by men, financially and professionally and emotionally, but now that her looks are failing, she's finding she has to actually like maybe do something.

I think I am supposed to feel sorry for her, or at least be able to put her into societal context. It was, after all, so hard to be a woman in that era. And she suffered so, in her childhood, from emotional neglect. Well, lady, I'm sorry but it's still hard to be a woman in society and everyone has their shit. I think briefly that this might be the fault of the biographer more than Rhys herself—biographers are forever trying to make connections, tease out the cause of each effect, root something ephemeral and divine in the mud of human experience, and many times they get it wrong. But the Rhys I find in the pages of the biography is repulsive to me.

I find myself unconsciously punishing the physical copy of the book for my frustrations. Never has such a book sustained so much accidental damage under my care. A cup of milky tea spills over its cover. While I'm reading in the tub it drops into the water. My hand slips as I read and the dust jacket tears. It looks as if I have given it a thrashing, as if all of the mental lashings have manifested physically.

Learning about Jean Rhys the person has changed how I see the books of Jean Rhys the writer. What I once saw as vulnerability I now see as passivity. What I saw as fragility I see as victimhood. What I saw as a clear-eyed view of society and its sexual dynamics I now see as self-serving justifications for bad behavior. Perhaps it was the revelation that despite writing incessantly about loneliness, Rhys always had a man on hand to buy her things, pay her rent, get her books published, put her up. Perhaps it is that her default mode was to lie on the floor in a puddle drinking until someone picked her up and pointed her in a specific direction. Perhaps it is that I have always seen this type of woman as my enemy.

Emma and I are out eating noodles, both of us longtime lonelyhearts. I knew her in New York, was neighbors with her in Berlin, and am now visiting her in London. I mention reading Jean Rhys's biography, and Emma immediately says, "Isn't it disappointing? You think a writer understands your loneliness, but then you learn she was never really without a man her whole life."

Yes. Yes it is disappointing.

* * *

I don't like London, I think as I walk three miles into town to meet up with my friend Margaret. *I don't like it,* I think as I worm my way through crowds and around sidewalk cafés and parks. It's so crowded, it's so money-driven, it's so expensive. I swear I can feel my bank account slowly emptying itself as I make my way through the city, and then all of a sudden I am standing next to Crispin Food & Liquor again.

It was another late night, another long conversation with the lover. He wants to come to London, he can't come to London. He has a new life to figure out, a new home to find, a divorce to finalize. "If I have a secret marriage, then I also have to have a secret divorce." I give him time, and I try not to let him pull on me. But it's hard to sleep in a constant state of expectation.

Which is why I need to see Margaret. Margaret fills my arms with books and my mouth with gin and my ears with gossip about the famous clientele at her bookshop and her amazing

New Zealand–tinted chortle as we find refuge from the heat and the people. "They want a second copy of my father's birth certificate."

"Who?"

"I'm renewing my visa. You know," she says slowly, as giant televisions light up behind her, all with the inexplicable act of cricket suddenly broadcast brightly, "I think it's possible my father was a spy. We found this stuff after he died."

"Maybe that will help you with your visa, you should put that on your application. Father's occupation: spy for the Commonwealth. They owe you that visa."

In the stack of gifted books is a story about a young woman in the city. She dies. Or maybe fakes her death. The detective investigating her maybe suicide becomes obsessed and makes a lot of pronouncements about where society is going. The death is a metaphor.

"They have this ad campaign here now," Margaret tells me, as our conversation moves on and I start wondering how I will make it back to my apartment all wobbly with gin, "about how you shouldn't take a cab unless you hire one over the phone. They had these posters of women looking vulnerable in the backs of cabs, saying, 'If your minicab's not booked, it's just a stranger's car,' or something."

"Jesus."

"Rape is inevitable for 80 percent of cab rides."

I decide to risk it, after walking into the Underground station and seeing how there would be three entire times I was going to have to get off the train at exactly the right moment and then get on one specifically correct train going in the right direction while other trains would be deliberately trying to deceive me into going in the wrong direction. This seemed more dangerous.

I get into the back of a stranger's car. He takes me directly home.

* * *

In the Very Bad Novel I got from Margaret, sometimes the dead girl is Lost Innocence, sometimes she is a World Gone Mad, other times she is the Sins of the Father. She gets swallowed up by the city and never finds her way back. She should have stayed in the gated community where she was protected. I look for the Rhys biography; somehow it is lodged between the bed and the wall, half of the pages now wavy and bent.

Jean Rhys came to London to finish her schooling, and she first saw the city through that schoolgirl misfit mentality. Coming from the islands, she had the wrong clothes, the wrong accent, the wrong hair. The other girls had money, she had a stingy aunt who didn't understand the importance of girlhood display. The importance of being homogenous and yet singular, fitting in with a twist. At any rate, Rhys had a miserable time, and switched to an arts and performance school because she was headed for a life on the stage.

Big dreams die hard et cetera et cetera, it is the storyline of many Lost Girl narratives. A girl knows she is meant for a life of glamour and fame, but the stage can support only so many bodies at a time. You get pushed back into the chorus line or the scenery and die in obscurity, or you end up in dark places trying to find your moment. But if you don't have that oomph, that pizzazz, that know-it-when-I-see-it-and-girl-I-just-don't-see-it thing, that magic you can't even work for because it is either bestowed or it is not, you're never going to make it. Rhys did not have it. She was stuck in revues and chorus lines, showing a little bit of flesh and a little bit of wiggle, and traveling around giving shows in depressing rooms.

So. What is the substitute here? Every desire is an arche-type, and we just spend our lives finding new variations that match up. Fame brings attention, it brings care. Fame lets you know you are important because people treat you like you are important. Worldwide fame was not to be Rhys's fate, but she could satisfy that craving, built by a mother who was too deep in mourning for children who had died to notice little Jean/ Gwen and by a typically distant father, through men. Anyway, men are easier to manage and draw in than an adoring horde. They give you attention in the form of gifts and sex, they care for you by putting you up in a better room and paying for your abortion. They let you know you are important by treating you like you are important.

And there is a certain type of man who rewards passivity, who needs to feel like the hero because of a weak mother or absent father or whatever particular dynamic creates that par-ticular man. Jean Rhys kept finding that man. Over and over again. And so her life story is one of passivity and childishness, of throwing tantrums when a man loses interest, in making scenes, in that so boring, so clichéd "Well, I'll just kill myself if you leave me," all said halfway out the window, but with per-fectly styled hair and dewy makeup, clothing in artful disarray and a tragic string of pearls. Performance is always required for this particular archetype. Being that girl is just another way of being a monster.

The disappointment of Rhys novels, now that I have seen their context, is that she was so little aware of this monstrous-ness. She had no awareness that this behavior reinforces the paternal, patronizing aspect of men, that this view of life is deeply cynical and toxic. And certainly I do not want all of the women in the books I read to be crime-fighting, tough-talking babes, I think that is just as mixed up and gross, but I don't know if this particular story needs to be told anymore. Maybe

I've just had too many interactions with these real-life girls to want them in my fictional material too.

When I'm done rereading *Voyage in the Dark* in a little café near the British Museum. I drop my copy onto the stack of dusty "take one leave one" paperbacks and walk out the door.

*　*　*

It has been known for a while that schizophrenia in urban areas is a chronic condition, a never-ending instability that requires constant care and management, while in rural areas and in traditional communities, schizophrenia is something one can recover from. It happens, and then one can mend. It's been known for a while that psychosis is more probable in cities. That immigrants are particularly vulnerable to it. There is a reality inside their minds, about how the world works and what the world consists of, and then there is a reality outside of them that contradicts and disproves this. We are not all entirely durable, some of us go slipping over the edge.

And London has been built on and with the blood of girls, from the raped daughters of Boadicea to the victims of Jack the Ripper. The Lost Girl is as archetypal as the Bad Man. And this dance they do for us, oh how we love it. We love to sing songs about it and write stories about it. We love to act it out in our own lives, displaying our vulnerabilities, crouching in the corner and waiting for the big bad wolf to materialize. And he will. Insist you are a harmless bunny for long enough, and your predator will appear.

That is my problem with the Lost Girl narrative. City life, life in general, is hard enough as it is. All of these girls, pretending they are born under the star of Persephone, playing out their Pluto as the (un)willing companion downward. These girls I have no time for.

And then an emergency signal in my e-mail. A colleague

traveling in Nepal is panicking over a canceled flight. One of the things I had been drawn to about this woman is that she had traveled the world. When I had learned the travels had been funded by various men and in their company, I found her much less interesting. That narrative is common, and cheap. But here she is out on her own for the first time, and her connecting flight home has been canceled, and she does not have a phone to call the airline.

"Can you do it? Get me rebooked for the next day?"

"I don't have a phone either, I'm traveling. I could call using Skype I suppose."

"Yes, that should work."

As I sit on hold for forty-five minutes, am disconnected in the process of being transferred, have to call back and sit on hold for another hour, I think about all the things she could have done to solve this problem herself. Her flight wasn't for several days, after all. She could have taken the bus to the airport to talk to the airline. She could have gone to a tourist office or a travel agent. She could have gone into one of the luxury hotels and spoken to someone who speaks English. Someone would have responded to her wiles. But when things go wrong during travel, if you're not used to it, your brain flashes DEATH INEVITABLE and does not always think creatively.

After four hours, I have her flight rebooked. I send her the confirmation codes. I look up and realize, her green Skype light has been on this whole time, she could have made this call herself. Could have, but didn't have to.

She writes back without even a thank you. "I wanted an aisle seat, my legs get so cramped. It would be really great if you could call them back and get me an aisle seat."

These girls. These girls who look away when the bill is presented, these girls who feign having no upper-body strength so that someone will carry their heavy loads, girls who scheme and use and lay waste to the people around them just so they will not be inconvenienced, these girls are poison. The girls for whom men lay out their money, the girls who get out of every bad situation of their own creation on the back of someone else. As I walk through this world, I collect these girls like sticky burrs, and once recognized they have to be removed.

"Sorry," I write back. "I just broke my headset and can't make the call. Just talk to the airline when you get to the airport Fly safe!" This was hardly the first time I'd found myself entangled with this woman. She did, after all, once refuse to attend a party being held in my honor because she thought it was unfair that the party was not in her honor instead. I delete her e-mail from my contacts.

But, I argue with myself, *are you just envious that you have no sexual currency to cash in? You, an Ugly Girl of Note? Because you will always be carrying your own bags, paying your own bills, you are just nasty about it because no one offers.*

Maybe. But I have learned to recognize when the strength of someone I admire came to them parasitically, and I do not respect their methods. And while I might not be beautiful and soft and alluring, by now, carrying my bag across Europe, I am strong, and my methods of acquisition are legitimate, and I refuse to have it drained off by my enemy, the Lost Girl (Posed).

* * *

Rebecca West reviewed Jean Rhys's *After Leaving Mr. Mackenzie*. She wrote, "Miss Jean Rhys has already, in *The Left Bank* and *Postures*, quietly proved herself to be one of the finest writers of fiction under middle age, but she has also proved herself to be enamoured of gloom to an incredible degree."

I don't like it when my dead ladies fight, but I agree with West's assessment. I also see how a woman who pretends to be stronger and more independent than she really is would recoil at Jean Rhys's performance of weakness. The biographer takes Rhys's side in this argument, hissing that West was just H. G. Wells's mistress and playing up how hurt Rhys was by this review. Even after her death, her fragility has everyone rushing to her side, to pet to coax to soothe.

Maybe I would be more forgiving of this behavior if I didn't understand it so well. The way women feign pain and weakness to force the world to take care of them in a way that the family could not or did not. Their sense of entitlement, which warps every interaction into a transaction. The justifications that spill out, about women's place in the world and the patriarchy and whatever, as if this performance were not in direct support of the patriarchy. This very feminine weapon, this weakness, the insistence on playing the role of the victim, so that the only role left for you is that of bully.

And then here is Jean Rhys, so desperately passive. Even her imagination retells only her own personal history in her books, it cannot possibly take on the act of creation. Wouldn't it be nice, you want to ask her, to desire something? To try for something? To use your wasted muscles and initiate forward motion? To do anything other than float along in the sea letting the waves and the currents toss you about?

Her biographer hisses at me, Spinster. Mistress. Bully.

* * *

Despite a few heightened e-mails, it is clear that the lover is not going to make it to London. I really am here on my own. In this city he loves but I do not. I was hoping his love would be contagious, would let me see something I am missing.

And then one day, I am out walking and it is raining. Not a gentle London misting but a down-to-your-underpants downpour. I race to the subway station, I will be late meeting my friend. I am going to have to face my fears and actually use the Underground.

I have never liked subways, I do not like moving through a city without being able to see where I am going and what is happening around me. I like trams, I like above-ground trains. But subways, where you are one place and then suddenly you are in another place altogether with no connecting information, seems too much like a psychotic break to me.

But here we are, suck it up, lady. I fish out the Oyster card bestowed upon me by the New Zealander, and I plot out my route. I take one train, I get off and get onto another train, I get off and get onto another train. And there is something in the swooshing, in the rushed walking, in the determination and intention of it all, that I start to feel so very competent. Look at me, big-city girl, not just lying down in the tunnel and finding myself unable to move.

On the way out, there is a woman struggling with her suitcase. I recognize her as kindred. The men push past her, no one offers to help. I walk past as well, and then backtrack. "Do you want some help? I can grab the bottom and we can get it up the stairs that way."

Her look of relief is immediate. "It's heavy, you don't have to," but I already am. She was not there pouting, sighing, playing kitten with the men walking past, she was doing it herself, just not very well. "I can't believe you stopped. None of the men stopped."

I want to say, That is because you are doing it wrong, the needing help. You are not appealing to their patriarchal nature where they see women as helpless and in a constant state of distress. You are not flashing leg oh so subtly, your tear-filled eyes remain unbatted. But instead I say, "Men are awful," and get her to the top of the stairs. I disappear back into the crowd.

The only way to combat that feeling of being overwhelmed, that *let's just stay in and order sushi delivery from this website* feeling, is movement. The only way to disprove that London is a cold immovable object made up entirely of Pret sandwich shops and Starbucks and ATM machines is through contradiction. That requires observation.

Jean Rhys complained that London was too impersonal, too uncaring, but there is that saying that one finds the London one expects, and, I think to myself cattily, Jean Rhys required that her needs be met by others, probably including her cities. But what if there is another explanation for that coldness, which is a feeling shared by so many. Small towns, and even smaller cities, have the possibility of routine. A feeling of recognition as you walk through the streets. You know this person, you know how they link up with others. London, with its infinite variables, its ever-shifting circumstances, is like trying to sort a mountain of seeds. Because London is endless, and no matter how many books about its history, its culture, its people will be written, it will never be encompassed, its secrets will never be fully revealed. An ocean of ink has been used to explain London, and none of it helps me understand this city.

Perhaps these cities, these cities that feel permanent, your Londons, your New Yorks, your Mexico Cities, your Tokyos, perhaps they have been here for so long that they have escaped space and time. They do not simply exist in this realm but in all realms. You are not standing in the London of today but in the London of forever, its pasts and its futures, real and imagined. Maybe that impersonal feeling doesn't come from indifference but is the same as the gods looking down from heaven regarding the humans looking down through their microscopes regarding paramecia. And we, trying to understand our cities, are the paramecia looking back up and thinking we see the unblinking eye of an omniscient God.

Understanding that then becomes the key to the city, and this massive block breaks itself up into individual units for me. The mob sorts itself out into individual people with their own hopes and needs and routines, each contained in their own reality. And moving between these units is not a linear act but an act of stepping from one parallel universe into another. And each moment has to be considered and understood, and the person who follows behind you, that person travels through their own moments. No wonder fragile minds splinter in these transitions. No wonder the weary and the predisposed begin fragmenting when they settle when there are so few natural markers to keep you oriented, so few realities to intrude with the reminder that this is not the only one.

We don't do well with infinity and endless possibility, and so we break things down into individual units and into stories. And then we accidentally believe in those stories, and we accidentally start acting them out. Stories about what love is, what happiness is. What men are, what women are. Unable to shape our own stories about the madness that surrounds us, we get infected with other people's stories, trying to ignore the discomfort that comes with an imperfect fit.

Maybe that's why I'm obsessed with this idea here, Londoners are always trying to explain themselves to themselves, to the world. Ever since the iconoclasts severed the tradition of art with their holy campaign of purity and abstraction, London was left with only words. And now, left without its nobility, what is the story of London? Is it just going to copy down New York's story about how money gets you everything you want, all you have to do is work hard enough for it? Is it going to be Paris and Gypsies get out, this is our country? The story that London tells is going to be the key to what happens next to it. It is going to have to figure it out.

God help me, I am beginning to like London.

* * *

In Celtic fairy tales, there are two roles for women: the bride and the hag. The bride is so beautiful that men give her anything she desires. She moves directly from the protection of the father to the protection of the husband. She wants not. But her story always ends somewhere around "Happily Ever After," a boring little fadeout.

The hag is the rejected, ugly creature. The woman who has to make herself wise and powerful or just passively die on the side of the road waiting for someone to offer aid. She works for what she acquires, she seeks and finds wisdom through struggle. And she may know all of the secrets and understand everything that goes on around her, including the movement of the heavens and the language of the fish in the river and which god you need to talk to for which problem; she will always be physically repulsive.

No wonder the hag is forever trying to mess with the bride. No wonder she says, "Fuck you little girl, here have a poisoned apple." To just have the world on offer rather than fighting for it. And then to take it for granted, to just sit there waiting for it to come to you, for disrespecting it in that way, fuck that girl. Poison her, put her in a tower, pull her beautiful hair.

Because even the Celts knew that it is beauty we envy, never wisdom.

* * *

Maybe my animosity toward Jean Rhys is simply misplaced animosity toward this nineteen-year-old version of myself. Would you stop cutting your own hair and what's with that stump? Are you seriously going to wear that cardigan you stole from your father, it's got a hole in the elbow. God, don't cry, I'm sorry, but also is that your response to all stimulus now? Open-mouthed weeping? It's not that bad, just stand up and wipe your nose you're leaking all over the place.

In the mystery novel the nineteen-year-old sidekick, beautiful and quirky, has fallen in love with the grizzled much older detective. She is Hope Regained. She is much less brilliant but less Troubled and manipulative than the victim, more Pure, less Sullied, and so she gets to live.

I think the lesson we are supposed to take away from these Lost Girl narratives is that the world is not safe for you. It is full of danger and predators and Downfall. Best then to stay home, where you are safe and taken care of, where you can retain your purity and your innocence, so that your parents don't have to one day come identify your headless body from the constellation of moles on your back.

We used to think homesickness was fatal, back when we believed in humors and all that. Our fluids would be so caught up pining for our blessed mother that they could not keep our heart pumping and our liver churning or whatever physical thing it does exactly, and our bodies would just give out. And I keep humming those ballads of country girls lost in the city, and I keep reading these Jean Rhys novels about helplessness and despair, and I wonder why we can't seem to find another fucking story to tell.

Not that the world is not dangerous for women. But eventually the statistics and the warnings and the news stories all become like those urban legends your mother forwarded to you the year you left for college about the man who will hide under your car and slice open your heel as you approach and you will bleed to death while he drives off. Or the other one, about the rapist, circling endlessly, who will hide in your backseat and then BOO and a knife to the throat and then you are damaged goods forever. It is hysterical manipulation.

And it is worrying that these are the stories we prefer to tell ourselves about how men are and about how women are.

A few years back, a young Englishwoman from a small town went off to Tokyo to find work and money, she was told that young blond hostesses could make a lot of money from lonely businessmen. She flirts, she engages in conversation, she laughs charmingly, and he hands over money. She ended up dead, snuffed out by some serial killer, and then a London journalist turned the story into a book. And it made for a ripping good read, a mother who had premonitions that her young daughter would die in Japan, the girl who always had the strange feeling she would die young, the city that eats its vulnerable young women.

The book was a hit. And why not, it's exactly the kind of story we like to tell. It was compared to *In Cold Blood*. The violence of the big city taking the innocence of the small-town inhabitants. I grew up not far from that town, and Kansans like to grumble about where Capote overreaches, about how his depiction of small-town innocence makes them all look like yokels. It's not like Kansans don't know darkness, don't know horror. It's just that this one time the darkness and violence and horror were sourced from outside the house, rather than from within.

* * *

I would guess that the story Jean Rhys was telling herself was about victimhood when it should have been about entitlement. Her family's story was one of colonialism, after all, a British white family in a position of power on a historically black island. Later Rhys would make slightly absurd statements about how not every white family mistreated their black servants, not seeing unbalanced power dynamics as mistreatment I guess. And when the story you are born into is that you get to use the people around you to get what you want, it's easy to fill in one type of person for another.

I go to get my tarot cards read at Treadwell's, just another part of London that occupies spaces in other realms than the physical. I need a new story to tell myself, something other than "I am in love and it is not working out because that really just never works out for me." The man is kind, I am a bit of a mess.

"Your relationship is a power struggle, not a friendship." I don't recognize the cards, he's using a Celtic deck and so I can't argue with the story he makes out of the images. "This relationship seems to be coming to an end."

I smear the cards around the table again, put them back together, and hand them to my reader. "But you have someone new who will appear in six to eight weeks. He has money. He can support you."

"Emotionally or financially?"

"Both."

Ugh. I already dislike it when people start using tarot cards to prognosticate, and he starts telling me who the handsome man is going to be, the one who will tell me where to live and fix my life. He's older, he's wealthy and so will be able to fund my dreams. I wonder if this is what the reader thinks I want to hear, that a man will come and make my decisions for me. I don't know if he knows I can fund my own dreams, even if mostly in a slapdash, paltry kind of way. I don't know if he knows work is the most important thing in the world for me. That does not seem to be showing up in the cards.

I thank him for his time, I pay him, and I leave disquieted. I go into the wine shop next door and buy three bottles, all from countries I have loved: Hungary, Ukraine, Germany. All countries I visited while paying for my own train tickets, my own sublets, my own bar bills. And I did that by working, all the time, for my own business. That man in the reading, I know, does not exist. And that story I wanted to be able to tell myself, that didn't really fit me.

I'm growing out of one story, but I haven't figured out the new one, not yet. Maybe then we're just in the story of the Tower, the state of breaking down before the rebuilding. For now, that will have to be enough. I have a plane to catch.

Jersey Island / Claude Cahun

No, I will follow the wake in the air, the trail on the water, the mirage in the pupil . . . I wish to hunt myself down, to struggle with myself.

CLAUDE CAHUN, *Disavowals*

"I don't even know what's in Jersey. I mean, I saw *The Others,* and I'm going to be very disappointed if it is not exactly like that."

"Ghostly children and fog?"

"Yes."

I was with Margaret on my last night in London, drinking bourbon and eating pastrami. "They have cows, right? Isn't that where the name of the cow comes from, the Jersey cow?"

"Oh!" It had never occurred to me. Jersey the place and Jersey the cow. I had always just pictured Brits with money sunning themselves on beaches. I suddenly felt much better. If all I had to do was journey to places with special cows for the rest of my life, I think I would be fine.

But here was the entirety of my knowledge about Jersey Island before my departure:

- Cows
- The movie *The Others* is set there, with Nicole Kidman running around looking distressed while wearing amazing outfits

- There were news reports about a school or a large foster family or some other grouping of adults that was abusing the children, feeding them bleach or keeping them chained in the basement, something like that
- It was the only British territory occupied by the Nazis during the war
- Claude Cahun lived there

Surely that is enough to know about a small island you'll be living on for a while. It's still British, and it's a small island. Neither of those things is unfamiliar. All small towns operate in a similar fashion, in that if you are not from there they don't really know what to do with you. I would be sure to drag along a lot more books and be ready to be eyed suspiciously. It would basically be like visiting my hometown, if Kansas suddenly developed a shoreline.

* * *

The first time I saw a photograph of Claude Cahun, I was reading the *London Review of Books* on a plane, and I mistook the woman in the photograph for Kathy Acker. It was the shaved head, the full mouth, the "go fuck yourself" look in the eye. As a teenage girl, I had collected all the Grove paperbacks of Acker's novels, each featuring a different author portrait on the cover, but all with the same stance, the same attitude. All leather boots and red lipstick, a punch to your face and a hand down your pants.

My first introduction, then, was conflation. The Cahun version of Acker had the shaved head, but angled to look frail and sickly, near death, a pre-Holocaust vision of the Auschwitz survivor. And yet a defiant lip, a gaze too furious to meet the camera directly. The power of it, the shock of it. And yet the first thing I thought was *All of us girls have been dead for so long.*

But we're not going to be anymore, a line from Acker's *Pussycat Fever.* It may as well have been captioned in red lipstick underneath.

Cahun was like Acker's sexless twin, because while there was the same aspect of performance and identity- and gender-fucking, and the use of the body to convey a message, Cahun's body remained closed off in her photos. It was like the picture of her dolled up in a grotesquerie of the coquette, a message scrawled on her chest that says, "I am in Training. Don't Kiss Me." All of her work gave off that message, the gendered, but not sexed, display.

Maybe there's something, then, to the fact that I found Acker as a virgin and Cahun in the throes of my slut days. Here is something else you could do, they suggest.

Koestler theorized there was a special department of divine providence that ensured the intersection of the right person and the right book. When I was fifteen, the gods sent me Kathy Acker's *Pussycat Fever.* I prefer to think of it as a divine act, because it was such an unlikely intersection for a teenage girl in rural Kansas, in a town without a bookstore, in a home without the Internet, in a school without one of those kindly mentors who see the child's potential despite her raised-by-wire-monkeys attitude and take her under a protective wing and feed her intellectually and emotionally I am always seeing in movies and television. But I have always believed in the gods, and the gods have always expressed themselves to me with books.

So at fifteen I came across a review of Kathy Acker's *Pussycat Fever* in a magazine called *huH,* which I think existed for approximately eight issues. Angelic choruses, unconscious drives, I don't know, for whatever reason because of a four-paragraph review, I sent a SASE to AK Press distro, requesting their catalog. When it came I circled the items that I wanted, including the Kathy Acker book. I counted up money from my after-school job at my father's pharmacy and purchased a money order at the local credit union and mailed it. In return, a large stack of books that rewired my brain arrived in Lincoln, Kansas.

I was ready for these books. I had filled up on the Brontës. I had experimented in self-harm. I had decided that there was no way forward for me, that I probably was not going to make it. And then Kathy Acker arrived. To say, here is something else you could do.

Not that she offered a cheery view of the world. Her stories are not stories of rosy recovery and spiritual awakenings and gentle lovemaking on a yoga mat. That wouldn't have connected. I didn't know how to enter the world as this bloodied, carved-up, traumatized amphibious creature. I didn't know we were allowed in, because I didn't have access to those stories. Acker's books, violent and sexual and profane and wonderful, those books knew me. Knew the bilious contents of my head and said yeah, over here too. Said that being alive and aware is yes, the worst thing ever. But death is too easy, too predictable. Put down the knife, honey. Or at least turn it on someone else.

* * *

When someone says a song or a book or a poem saved their life, this is what they mean:

- it took me out of my brain for the one second needed to get back onto the planet
- it shot out a spark into the distance that I could then build a path toward
- it opened something up in my imagination

Because suicide is the result of the death of the imagination. You forget how to dream up other possible futures. You can't picture new maneuvers, new ways around. Everything is just the catastrophic present and there will never be a time this is not so. That is what kills you.

What saves you is a new story to tell yourself about how things could be.

* * *

I was wrong about Claude Cahun, because she was not the solitary genius creating brilliant self-portraits that somehow captured the entirety of the soul of the twentieth-century individual that I had assumed she was. Had I stopped to think about it for a second, I guess it would have made sense to ask, Who physically took the pictures? If Cahun is both the model and the artist, who is it actually pressing that little button on the camera?

Claude Cahun and Marcel Moore were stepsisters, collaborators, lovers. They had met as teenage girls and became sisters when their parents married. By then they had already fallen in love, which did much to vex their family. Claude and Marcel were originally Lucy and Suzanne, but the androgyny suits the work better and it suits the people in the photographs better. Claude had been taking pictures of herself, experimenting with identity and gender and body, from a young age, but she thought of herself primarily as a writer. In Paris they worked together on the page and in the theater, with Claude as the flamboyant center of attention and Marcel always a little off to the side, drawing.

They moved to Jersey Island in 1937, leaving behind the surrealists and avant-garde of Paris. They remembered Jersey from childhood holidays, and maybe Jersey seemed like an escape from the madness of a Europe crawling toward war. The war and the madness would follow them. Perhaps it was also an escape from their peers. Androgynous or not, they were still women in an artists' clique tightly controlled by André Breton, and fellow surrealist outcast Leonor Fini reports that women who wanted to think and create, rather than just model and nod heads, were not welcome in Breton's gang. Or maybe it was just that shoreline, which sticks in your throat and makes you want to walk into the sea arms outstretched. Why meditate and fast to reach your ecstatic state when all you have to do is look out your window?

Cahun and Moore came to Jersey Island, and here they took photographs in their garden and on the shore. Cahun in front of the camera, Moore behind the camera. But: collaborating. The ideas bloomed in the space between these two women. And those ideas were recorded on film, allowing us to see them years later, despite the photographers' lack of interest in posterity.

* * *

I have rented a little room in a little house with a window that looks out to sea. The room receives no direct sunlight, and the cold sea air blows in and it is freezing despite the Indian summer. The woman who runs the place, tall, imposing, sings Whitney Houston songs around the house in the voice of a turkey that was taught human speech and is now being stabbed to death, does not care and refuses my requests for a space heater or at least an extra blanket. I must warm myself with scotch.

And anyway, it's worth it, I tell myself as I start putting on all the clothing from my suitcase the moment I wake up. I walk outside and I am under the hot sun. Two blocks and I am at the sea. At low tide it looks like an alien landscape, with sharp rock structures revealed and the strange coils of the remnants of lugworms dotting the sand. And at high tide it is crashing and roiling and all drama-queen natural beauty. I suddenly want it to be autumn so I can walk along here with an oversized cardigan, drinking hot coffee spiked with whiskey while the wind blows the salty mists through my hair, also then if it were autumn maybe they would turn the heat on in my room.

It is a two-mile walk from the little house into St. Helier, and then a bus to get to where Cahun and Moore lived. But at least the walk can mostly be done along the shore, so I don't mind. The beaches on this side of the island are quiet, and there is almost never anyone at the market. Outside my window, magpies play at destruction. Three of them land on the roof and start tugging at the shingles with their beaks. They do not seem to be trying to get at something under the rooftiles, they are simply being willful little hooligans. They manage to pry one off and toss it around between them, before flying off with their wicked cackles.

* * *

And I mean, it's kind of a great story. That's part of why I am here, for the story. Here are these two middle-aged lesbian artists hanging out on an island, and then here come the Nazis. And these two women, instead of just keeping their heads down or trying to rally the inhabitants of the island to revolt, they decide they'll go after the Germans themselves. Not all of the Germans can be rabid Nazis, they think. They write hundreds of leaflets in German—which apparently they don't speak so much, as I discover when I start to translate the surviving documents with a Berlin friend over Skype: "They write German like you write German," she tells me—in the voice of a German soldier, *der Soldat ohne Namen,* who urges his comrades to mutiny.

Being skilled pickpockets and socially invisible, they slip the propaganda into the pockets of the occupiers. They write letters as the ghosts of dead soldiers. They particularly like pamphleting the funerals of dead German soldiers, writing in the voice of the recently deceased. Their house is right next to the cemetery, and yet no one suspects them. They dress up in costumes and take on new identities to sneak around the island. They try to wake up the Germans to what they are really doing and how this will all end badly. Some Germans start to desert and disappear off the island.

The Germans in charge start to get nervous. They figure that this must be a well-organized movement of dozens of people. And not, you know, two ladies who live by the sea. The Germans start searching for this resistance movement, and meanwhile the two ladies sit and write their propaganda: The Allies are making headway, Berlin is burning, there is no hope for you, get out while you can. They get away with this for four years.

And then they are arrested and sentenced to death.

The thing I can't figure out is why this story is not more often told. When I mention Cahun to associates, their eyes are blank. When I start to tell this story, the story of what she and Moore did during the war, they lean forward and get excited. "But that is amazing, why have I never heard of her?" I can't figure it out. I wonder, if she painted harmless little watercolors of the sea, maybe she would have her own Spielberg biopic by now. He could turn her straight, or Moore would be Sister, not Lover. A heroic woman standing up to bullies? While her own peers collaborate or at least turn a blind eye to the occupying force in Paris? (There is Coco Chanel's Nazi lover, there is Jean Cocteau's kind words about Hitler's friends, there is Gertrude Stein being an unbelievable fucking monster.) Surely there is an American actress ready to accept the Oscar just waiting for this role.

Or maybe it's that Cahun is a cipher, her inner world a mystery to us. What we know of her is her outer self, these pictures where she's playing hide-and-seek with the camera. And for a story to travel, it needs to be relatable. People need to imagine they can step into that place, occupy the narrative. Genius trans-everything lesbian outsider approximately a hundred years ahead of her time with an inexhaustible source of compassion and courage . . . No one is going to read that and say, *Oh yes, just like myself.*

But also, treating German Nazi soldiers as if they have the potential for compassion and rational thought, no one wants to watch that.

* * *

I walk into St. Helier, taking the route around the castle, to meet with Louise Downey, the Jersey Heritage's art curator. I've seen the island's collection. It is some nice society portraits, a few striking Victor Hugos from his time spent here in exile, and then the exploding weirdness of Claude Cahun. Here her face is gold, here her body is painted. Here her face is replaced by flowers. Here her body is emaciated and curling. Here it is folded to fit into the drawer of a cupboard. Here she is a man, here she is a young girl. Here she is a god.

"They were thought eccentric," Louise tells me, referring to everyone else on the island. It wasn't the lesbian thing. "They were thought to be sisters more than lovers." But they would walk their cats on leashes, they invited artists over to the island for parties. No one really knew about the photographs, except the shop that developed the negatives. They kept to themselves.

She uses the word *sisters* to describe the couple so frequently that I am beginning to wonder if I made up the lesbian thing in my head. I say lovers, she responds with sisters. In the museum's collection, the materials refer to them as "The Surrealist Sisters." Even the little booklet I picked up about the German war cemetery uses the word *sisters*. It's not something I can account for easily, as downstairs from the Cahun collection the museum has in its historical section the tuxedos of the first gay couple to be legally married on the island. I can't point a finger and scream HOMOPHOBIA. Perhaps it's the combination of stepsisters and lovers, that incestuous whirl. Maybe they had to choose one, and the sisters thing has a paper trail and is more difficult to deny. But as emotionally tied in to one another as they were, it's a nasty bit of erasing.

"And then of course," she continues, "it was someone from the island who turned them in to the Nazis. We think. It would make sense if it was someone from the stationery shop. They wrote their propaganda on this very thin paper . . ." Her voice trails off, and I can imagine the rest.

We drink our coffee out in the glorious sun, and I ask her if Cahun is very popular at the museum. "Oh yes," she says, rattling off the major city museums that have requested loans of her materials. That's not what I mean. I mean, with the visitors. She pauses and looks into her coffee. "We have people who come specifically to see her work, like yourself. But the people who come to Jersey for vacation are not the type of people who would be generally interested in her work." She circles around the implication, that even fifty years on she's still the wild one, that after Cindy Sherman is turned into postcards and even my parents have seen the Marina Abramovic documentary, Cahun has not been incorporated.

The ugly, if popular enough, becomes beautiful. The shocking becomes mundane. As much as I want to keep these photographs covered, to protect them from familiarity, from that yawn of recognition when we see a van Gogh, from all of those Jersey Islanders who somehow don't spend every minute of the day on their knees, arms lifted in a hallelujah to that shoreline, I also want to protect her from the academy, the only place where she seems to be recognized at the moment. When I try to research her life and work, I get an eyeful of links to academic journals, thousands and thousands of words written by gender theorists. But god save us all from identity politics. Cahun was exploding her identity, not defining it.

Cahun still inspires revulsion, and perhaps that is why I can't stop looking at her. I want to give her image to every teenage girl taking selfie after selfie, trying desperately to convince herself she is not ugly, every teenage girl wanting to take a knife to the source of the image. Trying to find the one angle they won't recognize themselves in, so they can sneak up on themselves as if for the first time and see their own face through a different lens from disgust. Yes, I want to say. But here is something else you can do.

* * *

And I can see them, Claude and Marcel, wearing the wigs and costumes they used to dress up Cahun for their portraits, taking the bus into St. Helier to slip messages of doom into the pockets of German soldiers. I can see them laughing as they hear rumors of a well-organized, well-populated resistance.

* * *

When I get back to the boarding house from the museum, there is news from home. A childhood friend, a boy, or I guess man now, took a gun and shot a man dead. Drugs, a woman, money—Mark, my oldest friend, and I e-mail back and forth and speculate on motive. We talk of him as an adult, as a murderer, and yet I can only picture him eight years old, when he'd bring his dog Pepper and his brother Kurt and hang out in my backyard, climbing the apricot tree behind the garage or sneaking into the abandoned house across the street. Red hair, freckles, ripped and grimy T-shirt. I picture that boy picking up a gun and ending all the other options of his life. It doesn't really matter in which direction that gun is pointed—the effect is nearly the same.

It's the same act, murder and suicide. A brain that fixates, and then the annihilation of a future. I don't know what to do with this information, I don't know what to do with my gothic past. I catch up with Mark, now living in Zambia, living a life he never would have guessed at. We kept each other alive, I think, when there was no future to imagine other than *out, out, out.*

I keep reading this anthology of true crime from Jersey Island, and it is filled with small-town despair. I recognize the crime templates from my childhood. Fueled by alcohol and loneliness and depression. Husband against wife. Son against father. Mother against children. People put into impossible situations, and instead of simply walking away, they explode. But then how does one walk away from an island?

A small town pens you in. It gives you a context and a place. It knows your name and your history. It knows how you correspond with the others around you. And either this will feel cozy or it will feel like suffocation. In the city you can construct your own identity from scratch. No one knows your past failures, no one knows what you looked like splayed out on the floor of the gymnasium in the seventh grade, your tooth knocked out and blood down your chin. You choose with whom you will correspond, how you will be represented, how you will be shaped. And either that will feel liberating or it will feel like schizophrenia.

But in a small town, so many of your options preselected for you, knock a few of the others out with bad decisions, bad luck, bad input from others, and the walls can close in all the more quickly. Because as long as you are in that town, your roles will never change. Son, father, neighbor, Lutheran, town drunk. The cast is set until death. And suddenly having to imagine a whole other way of being—it's not a course correction a lot of us can make.

And when you live in a place walled in on all sides, all of your life must feel it is blockading you in as much as keeping the invaders out.

Jersey wears its wariness of strangers on its perimeter, in its fortifications and seawalls and castles and towers and batteries It
exists in enemy territory, nudging right up close to the French
coastline. And it acts like it, wearing its armor to the dinner
table the way that it does. Jersey is still sensitive about the time
the French tried to take the island, it is the subject of an ever-
looping documentary at the Heritage foundation. The invasion
battle lasted half an hour or so, but maybe those thirty minutes
still echo in the hearts of its inhabitants.

Do not, the sign at the post office says, dare to try to use a
postage stamp from Guernsey Island, Jersey's sister, which is
just over there, off to the side. They don't say what will happen,
but I imagine them spitefully burning the misstamped letters in
the back. Walking from one side of the island to the other, you
move over this richly guarded land. You start with the yachts of
the wealthy and move quickly to the cows. And the cows are
wonderful. Docile and polite, with velvety eyes and movie-star
lashes. But even if you are trying to move slowly, soon you have
passed the farmland and the occasional dots of houses and then
you are back to seashore restaurants and fortifications and the
sea.

The map of Jersey lists eight separate forts, more than a
dozen fortified towers, and a smattering of German-built batteries and turrets, for an island that is approximately forty-five
square miles. I imagine the suicidal brain, if its metaphors were
represented visually, would look a great deal like Jersey Island.
All of these towers and walls and borders. All of the forts and
castles and complicated entryways. And the suicidal brain will
say, *This is for your own good. It is for your protection.* And it will
believe what it is saying.

The suicidal mind, wandering out into the world, is indeed

butting up against hostile enemies. People who can disappoint you, men who can reject you, opportunities that can be denied. And that mode, of depression or anxiety or psychosis or PTSD, it is all about protection. (But if we asked and it was forced to answer, protection from what? it would have to say, Hope.) Because once before it could be properly dealt with you were disrupted and jarred, and the brain says, never again. And so it must go about shutting down the potential dangers, even the one that closely resembles a hand extended. And it shuts them all down until that final act of protection, the murder of the self.

* * *

Cahun died soon after the war of ill health. Moore died by her own hand. She was left alone on an island that had betrayed her to the Nazis, she had lost the subject of her photographs. There were perhaps other futures she could have had, moving back to Paris maybe. Showing someone the work they had been doing in private. Finding a new subject. Either she couldn't imagine it or she knew it could never be as nice as being in that seaside house with the person she had loved since she was a girl.

Death's appeal and advantage is its obviousness. Its big, blocky stop. Whatever else might happen at the end of all of it, at least this particular existence with this particular brain and this particular circumstance is over. The rest—eternal boredom in heaven, maybe, or being sent down for another go-around—can be dealt with as long as this particular identity ends.

One of my favorite portraits is of Cahun lying in the sun, eyes closed. The light is at Marcel's back, and across the side of the portrait, her shadow lies down beside Cahun.

* * *

Cahun and Moore's photos were found after Moore's suicide, which followed Cahun's death by almost twenty years. Moore's estate had come up for auction, and when the belongings were to be cataloged, these stunning photographs and negatives were found lying about on the floor, shoved in cardboard boxes, fallen behind a dresser. One had been caught under a door and swept along the dusty floor as it was opened and shut.

Eventually the collection ended up at the Jersey Heritage, and I went and filled in my request to view a few items. Among the photos and the negatives and a few stray pages of the propaganda and a letter from a British friend dated after the war asking why in the world are you still on the island filled with the people who turned you over to the Nazis is a letter in German. It's from a German soldier who was on Jersey, but it's impossible to find out any more information about his identity. He's in hospital, in custody of the British, and he wanted to say hello. The weather here is fine, I hope this finds you well.

Had Cahun or Moore been recognized as lesbians, their executions would have come swiftly, but apparently two middle-aged ladies living together did not read to the Germans as "lesbian." They were also ironically saved by their dual suicide attempts after they were first incarcerated, both of which failed but left them too sickly for transport. And so they waited out the nine months in the island prison, finding a way to pass each other letters, watching prisoners of war come in and then go out never to be seen again, making conversation with German traitors. They lived through it.

* * *

I am lost in the cemetery. I am looking for Cahun's and Moore's gravestones, but they are eluding me. The cemetery and church overlook this bay and are directly next to the house they shared, now marked with a small plaque. From their garden they could see a beautiful expanse of seaweed and sand, rock and water. They had always taken their pictures, but once they made it to this island the pictures started being set more often outdoors. One can see why.

But today I can't find their bodies. The church has a coffee shop attached, and I go in to ask for directions. The woman, though, when I say Cahun's name, shrugs. "Sister Margaret will be here tomorrow after services, you could ask her then. What year did she die?"

"1954."

"Ah, then the cemetery up in the front may still have been the German war cemetery. She might be in the plot in the back." But even in the back, I can't find them. It feels rude, stomping over buried bodies, studying melted marble headstones that retain only the faintest outlines of names and dates, looking for two particular dead women and disregarding the others.

A man from the coffee shop approaches as I stumble around the yard. "Did you find her?" He speaks with a thick Austrian accent. "Who is she again? Is she family?"

I want to claim her as kin, but no, just an artist who lived here during the war . . .

"Ah! The artists!" He vaguely remembers the story and knows vaguely where the marker will be. We move to the right of the church and study headstones together. "My family came here after the war," he tells me, and I'm wondering if he's wondering if I was wondering about his wartime tie to the island. "But I remember, there is the Star of David on the top, that is what we must look for. The only Jews in this cemetery." We split up, and after several minutes I hear him call my name. He is grinning and pointing down. I hurry over.

He touches my arm and then silently leaves me. I should have brought flowers. Or . . . something. I wasn't really prepared for this, I am not a grave site pilgrimage person. Can I leave a stone, or do I have to be Jewish to do that? Instead I touch the cool gravestone with my fingertips. "Thank you," I say.

A fortified island, a fortified brain, labels everything that appears outside of it Monster or Invader. Threat, at the very least. It is all one deadly mob. I can't imagine the humanity and compassion it would take to look at the German soldiers who have occupied the island and are shipping their neighbors off to their death, have set up slave labor camps, and are waging war against the entire world, what it would take to look at those uniformed men and say, I bet there is a flicker of humanity left in there somewhere. And then make moves to nurture it.

* * *

After days of searching, I finally find a bookstore on the island. It is farther up the shopping street than I usually go; I normally detour the block before for coffee. Cahun had thought of herself as a writer first, and so I want something by her to read. There are a couple of her books in English in print, and I imagine that a place without a large, admirable literary legacy will be proud of its adopted daughter. She fought the Nazis and lord knows the British are still obsessed with the Nazis. She should get a display at the bookstore.

But first I have to search out my lover's novel. It is the first thing I do upon entering any bookstore. Not in some sort of ritual of love and devotion, but because coming across his name by accident does things to me. I can't imagine the sensation would be any different from running into your murderer casually on the bus. My throat thickens, alternating hot and cold needles dart into the back of my neck, everything below the knees disappears. If I can control the encounter by seeking him out and preparing myself in advance, I can control the reaction. I go to fiction.

In this odd little store, though, I can only find *A–F*. The fiction collection ends with Fowler. I search upstairs and down, looking for the other half of literature. Nothing. At least I can't run into the lover, and at least Cahun makes the cut, or would do if she could be found under *C*, and she cannot. But who knows where she might be stored.

"Excuse me, do you have anything by or about Claude Cahun?"

"Who?" The woman at the counter is not even looking up. She is wearing a whimsically colored eyeglass chain and a red poncho, and doing very important work on a piece of paper in front of her.

"She was an artist, she lived here."

Without moving her head, she waves me to Local Interest. There are a lot of self-published novels and short story collections, a book of local folklore, that true crime compendium I can't stop reading, a book about knitting . . .

You would think she would dominate, but I too hail from a small town. I know how they like to rewrite their histories to fit what they would like to have happened. I know that queer eccentric artists who shamed the local population by being the only visible resistance to the occupying force don't really fit into their timelines. Small towns see what they want to see.

*　*　*

In the morning I take Erich Fromm's *The Fear of Freedom* down to the dining room and order my breakfast. The book is not as much entertainment during the wait for my full English to arrive as it is a shield from the other occupants. The nice German couple has left the boarding house, and the only residents remaining as the late summer tips into off-season tell the same two stories over and over: how they almost couldn't land on the island due to the fog and circled the island forever and only had eight minutes of fuel for the circling remaining before they'd have to turn around and return to London when—a miracle!—the fog parted just enough to allow them to land. The other story involved a grandson's football match. I had both memorized, the pauses, the emphases, the cadences. I keep my head bent over my book.

The conversation lowers in volume, and I look up to see one of the couples, the ones with the flight story, glancing over at me as they are whispered to. I suddenly realize that I am not the mysterious stranger in the breakfast room, silent and alluring. I am the crazy spinster outsider, wearing the weird outfits and shoveling sausage after sausage into her face. How dreadful, I think. Although I could always embrace it, start bringing a cat down on a leash with me, feed her my fried egg on a saucer. Read to her out loud from the Fromm.

It's fine being the weirdo in the room, it's something I've had decades of experience with. But there's that moment when you realize you didn't even have the opportunity to reject them before they rejected you. I wonder if people who don't have that deep feeling of rootedness in their childhood are ever able to find a place that suits them. If you are displaced and shaken from birth, maybe it just never clicks. You read stories of people who flee to the city and find their "tribe," their spiritual home. I've been around the world and have never had that moment in any of my cities. Maybe you have to stay longer than a month. Or maybe I'm one of those plants you can hang from the ceiling and they live on air.

It wasn't so much that Jersey was Claude and Marcel's spiritual home as it was that their house was their spiritual home. They were each other's spiritual home. Cahun once wrote, "When we had cut loose from our world, I said: I am doing what I would rather be doing more than anything else . . . with the person I'd rather be doing it with." Maybe that's enough. Maybe I am looking for too large a scale. What if all I really need are a few square feet? But that seems easier to miss. Turn your head the wrong way as you are passing through and you'll never find it. But if you do find it, maybe what is whispered about you over baked beans and bacon will never matter again.

* * *

Then again, I am probably overly sensitive to always being the visitor and never being the native. The next morning at breakfast, the same couples say to one another: "I so like it here. But the people who live here . . . they're not very friendly are they?"

* * *

The question is, who is Claude Cahun, and I can't get a fix on it. We know who she is as a golden god, as a starving Buddha, as a dandy, but who is Claude, or Lucy? The young woman who ran away to Paris with her lesbian lover, shaving her head and taking a man's name? The middle-aged housewife who stood up to the Nazis? The radical feminist writer who took on the voice of the Virgin Mary, Judith, Cinderella to write about herself? What is the narrative thread that connects these different creatures? I can't find it, and no one else has done it convincingly. There is no real Claude Cahun biography, just an untranslated French bio that makes her sound like a lunatic.

Our culture has become obsessed with the I and mapping out our internal qualities, all while arguing that individuation is the first step to becoming a good member of a community, that the personal is universal, blah blah blah. And yet we have not from our little armies of unique individual spirits created a whole universe of equality and harmony and friendliness. We have separated out into our own divisible units, into our own one-and-a-half-bedroom apartments, and the only things we seem to share are pictures of what we are eating for dinner.

So I worry that every time I hit that I key (god, it never

stops), I am burrowing deeper and deeper into my viscera, that I am retreating so far into myself I'll never see daylight again. Like the silly child who wants to go to China and so digs a hole in the backyard instead of just getting on a plane. The only thing that will save me, or any of us, from our loneliness and despair is a sense of community and society. Those of us without family ties long for kinship, long to be recognized. The act of writing, the act of fleshing out our wintry family trees with the philoso-phers and storytellers and androgynous weirdos who have at one point or another saved our lives, is an important one.

Maybe the trick is not to define yourself as a container for your experiences, your thoughts. Maybe it's to assume you are larger than the things you have felt over a series of years, that your history is not a list of things your body has done or been present for, that your family is not people who you spent a lot of time around as a child or carry your genetic code. Maybe the trick is to push violently at your own boundaries, to find your own contradictions, and use your teeth and nails to destroy what separates you from something else.

I am trying.

Coda / Zakynthos

How did I end up back here? Somehow I am back at the same Paris subway station, trying to catch the same train to the same airport, the same terminal, flying eastward again. Only this time the stupid ticket machine won't take my credit card, nor does it accept bills. I just spent several minutes pouring every coin I had into the machine and I am 50 cents short of the €9.50 fare and now there is a line of pissed-off Frenchmen and women behind me and there is no gentleman to ask if he has any change.

The guy behind me asks in English, "What is the problem?" and I think, *Oh, guy, how long have you got*, but as I ask if he has 50 cents I can borrow, all of the coins I just deposited come spilling out again in a noisy flood.

I am about to abandon my task and maybe take a taxi instead, they'll take my cash, but the man deposits his credit card into the machine, and the machine is much friendlier to him. The machine is French, his card is French, you know how the French electronics are. I try to press the twenty-euro bill into his hand, but he waves me away. "The fare is only ten, it's too much." Yes, but you are my hero I want to say to him, but he says, "It's a company card, it does not matter."

He disappears into the crowd, and I make my way to the train platform.

I have spent the last two weeks in Lyon with my lover, now that he is post-moving out and mid-divorce. He showed up at the restaurant, ordered wine and cured meats, holding a bouquet of flowers, and when he touched my hand there was that rush downward and I cursed my body for the betrayal.

There were questions asked, answers received, and yet somehow it is all the more confusing, all the more tormented. *I am tormented*, I think to myself as I stand on the train platform. Tormented and yet heading to Athens.

"Meet me in Chicago," those were the parting words, or at least the last words I remember. After I am done with all of this, whatever this is, the plan is to meet him back in the city where it all started, a full circle of sorts.

A circle is too simple geometrically, after all of the looping backward on myself I've done. A full scribble. The kind done on walls by children, the kind that gets you yelled at. I never scribbled on my walls, that was my sister. Apparently I threw strawberries, though, frozen and then thawed, and watched them dribble down. I got yelled at for that, too.

God, my head is a mess. I'll be surprised if they let me through the Aegean Airlines security, if they don't pull me out of line for exhibiting obvious signs of mental illness. I haven't slept in god knows how long. It's always in these liminal spaces, on boats and trains and in airports, all of these boundaries between water and sky, earth and sea, when the uprooting has to happen for the motion to take place, that I lose it the most. I do my best crying at airports. Indoor sunglasses, a wistful stare, and snot running down my face. It is almost cinematic.

I am not sure what is more daunting: the journey to reach the Greek island I'm heading to (a train, a train, a plane, a taxi, a bus, a ferry, a taxi) or the idea of trying to establish a home again. This trip is almost over a year and a half of living out of a small suitcase, a year and a half of no permanent address or place to return to. All of my things are in a storage unit in Berlin. I hope my alabaster bust of Richard Wagner is not too scared of the dark. I hope he's not squabbling with my portrait of W. Somerset Maugham.

I am going to put off thinking about "home" as long as I can. I remember sitting in the sun in Paris with my friend John a few months ago, as we discussed *The Odyssey*. "Remember," he told me, "Odysseus steps back onto Ithaka halfway through the book. Half of the story is the journey. It takes just as long to get home as it does to come home."

* * *

This is the concern over the loved one who wanders: How will we ever get them to settle again? The experience will change them, they will see such marvelous things. And when they come back, will they suddenly see the limitations and deficiencies of the space around them with their new eyes? Once they have more, how will this small bit ever be enough again?

And there will be a distance. All of these spaces between us. Which is not to say that those distances didn't exist before, of course they did. But now we have to admit they are there, because they are filled with specific things. Experiences and stories. Images. Sounds and smells.

If you travel alone, no matter how hard you try, you can't share these moments with another person. You can sit your friend or lover down to an endless slideshow of your journey, tell them the stories that made you laugh or cry, and they will love you and they will try, but to them it's just a story. You are lit up with your history, and they are watching you light up. And it is so lonely, on both sides.

I have been both, the leaver and the left. And sometimes, when the physical distance has finally been reduced again, when you are holding your adventurous friend's hand at the bar and trying to follow along, sometimes that other distance, it can't be closed. Sometimes that friend stops showing up at the bar, sometimes you do too.

A man once told me: It's either me or this trip you are taking to Buenos Aires.

I chose Buenos Aires.

Someone expanding their life like that, it can make your life seem so small, especially if you had been feeling a bit restricted, pulled in at the seams, before the first slide went up. It doesn't help to explain, That's how I felt when you got married, all of this empty space beside me. I was happy for you and not. I danced at your wedding and cried in the bathroom. But wherever the empty spaces are in your life, they feel so much more gaping, so much more physical, than the empty spaces in your friend's.

"Yeah, but you got to go on a big adventure," say my loved ones when I wasn't there for their birthday or their Christmas or to see their children between the ages of three and eight. When I wasn't there.

As if it is not also possible to feel the absence of stillness, of calm. Of someone to ask you not to go.

Even if you'd go anyway.

*　*　*

A train, a train, a plane, a taxi, a bus, a ferry, a taxi. It is Zakynthos, not Ithaka. Let's not get literal about it, is my thinking. At least I have stopped crying, upon arrival the excitement of a new land outdoes the fear. At the place I was leaving, I had to grieve lost friends, lost grocery stores, lost dude who stood under my window every day for a week playing the theme song to *Brazil* on the clarinet. But here a whole new display of new friends, new grocery stores, new morning routines presents itself.

It is the beginning of the end of the tourist season, and so that loud, monotonous buzz of tourist appeal—cruise tours! bus tours! English breakfasts and American hamburgers so you'll never have to experience a moment of discomfort or unfamiliarity!—is quieting down. The blanket uniformity is ebbing away, the signs for scooter rentals, snorkeling lessons, lunch specials, the same signs that you'll find in any beautiful and poor spot in the world, they're coming down and the town is coming back to itself.

My driver explains which restaurants will be closing soon for the season and where I'll still be able to find food. It is day two of the US government shutdown, and apparently it is the subject of the radio news program, because the driver turns up the Greek official-sounding chatter, cackles, and says, "All this time, you have said Greece is the worst place, it does not work at all. Now you do not have a government! Where did your government go?" He bursts into fresh laughter.

I laugh along with him. I ask if he is from this village, but no, he is from a village on the other side of the island.

"This used to be very quiet, very quiet. No one came here. Then everyone had money and people came from England, from Germany. People borrowed money and they opened these stores for the tourists." He gestures out the window, every third storefront has a display of cheap sunglasses, inflatable pool toys, souvenir T-shirts. Large racks of sunscreen and bug spray. "Now no one has any money, people are not coming so much." And the street is quiet, there are only a few pale couples wearing shorts and sandals, walking in the hot sun. There are more stray cats visible than humans.

"Where are you from?"

"Chicago."

"Chicago! Are you a gangster?"

"Yes."

He laughs, and I laugh along with him.

Here I am at my home away from home, the eightieth time I have unpacked this suitcase, hung up this dress, laid out the yellow seashell and the flat gray rock that come with me wherever I go.

The room is small, with two small beds and one small desk with chair, and no shower, just kind of a faucet at chest level. There is a balcony that overlooks the sea, with pomegranate and orange and olive and lemon trees in between. It is perfect.

* * *

I don't want to think about Penelope. About how everyone in love is in some way Penelope, how we are all waiting at one time or another for our lover to come back to us. We sit at our desks, working and then undoing that work, marking time and waiting for the return of the one we love.

I am waiting for my lover to come back to me, for him to realize that the distance between my life and his is not a gap, it is an invitation. He is waiting for me to find the speed at which my life makes sense to me.

But it is hard not to want to feminist-overcorrect the story, let her get laid maybe. Smack her son for his bullshit silencing of her. And I am not passive, god fucking damn it. I am a verb. Yet here I wait on my Greek island. The image of Penelope is so perfect, of holding fast. Fidelity, in whatever way it is expressed. Fidelity, in the form of genital policing, has never meant so much to me. But the waiting for safe return, that I can do.

"Have you been seeing anyone?" he asks me as we talk over Skype.

"That's really none of your business."

He pauses. "That's all right. But when I get back, I am going to slay your suitors."

* * *

The family who runs the hotel, they live downstairs. A man, a woman, their adult son. There is some confusion as to my name, I say Jessa, they hear Chesska. I say Jessa, they hear Francesca. I let it be Francesca. I mishear their names, too, until the man writes them on the red tablecloth with his finger.

I am invited in for lunch, and lunch is a giant pile of garlic mashed potatoes and greens, fresh tomatoes, all drowned in oil, and tiny salty fish. They make the olive oil from the grove of trees that grow above their house. They also make their own wine, and they are generous with it.

Shit, I'm drunk. I'm drunk and everyone can tell I am drunk. I am drunk and it is 1 p.m., I should be ashamed. It is not my fault. The man just kept refilling my glass every time I took the smallest of sips, I can't even keep track of how much I drank. The wine is good—rough, but fruity and with bite. Up in my room I am drinking the table wine that comes in a big plastic jug from the place—it would be exaggerating to call it a winery—further into the island. It costs three euro, I am not criticizing in any way this family's wine it is delicious. Shit, I am drunk, aren't I? I need a nap.

The son is asking if instead I would like to come harvest walnuts with them. He is the only one at the table who speaks English, so his voice is the voice of God here. Yes, sure. How do you harvest walnuts? It is easy, he tells me. I should get a hat, I say, and I go upstairs for sunglasses and hat.

I am wearing the wrong clothing for harvest, I am wearing a sundress and halfway up the hill I remember I am not wearing underwear. I'll just have to make sure I am always downhill from everyone else. The son instructs me on the procedure. I am to take this big stick, and then go up to the walnut tree and bang it with the stick.

Walnut harvest is the best drunk activity I can think of. Out in the sun, sweating out the booze, hitting things with sticks and not even really requiring any sense of accuracy, it is tremendous. The walnuts rain down, but the wine numbs the discomfort of being pelted with nuts. The man escorts me to sit under the shelter, shaded by twisted grapevines, and he brings me walnuts that have dried in the sun to eat.

I watch the men repeat the procedure with new trees, the laying down of the nets, the introduction of the big stick, the whacking of the tree, the thundering showers of walnuts, green and large as tennis balls. The son's hair is beginning to speckle with gray, and his body is sleek and nimble under the walnut trees. As he raises his arms above his head to make a strike, his T-shirt lifts just a little to reveal a sliver of warm skin above his jeans.

I need to lie down, I think.

As the son drives me back down the hill, he thanks me for my help. Patronizing, but cute. "Anytime you need someone to hit things with sticks, I am your girl."

* * *

Would this be easier or more difficult with a home to come back to? Knowing that there's nowhere else to go and no one to take me in, that can make a person bolder and more timid all at the same time. Knowing you are accountable only to yourself, in that both you have to correct your own mistakes and yet your mistakes hurt no one else—it pushes and pulls.

When I've traveled before, with a place to come back to, the romantic notion I kept alive in my head of the morning light through the windows or watching the snow fall while staying safe and warm, of the place filled with friends and music, of laughter and conversation, it yanked me backwards. And I was surprised, every time, after I either cut a trip short or spent days of it longing for my own bed, to return and find my place cold, the mattress as lumpy as ever, my friends elusive.

I always long for the place where I am not. When I am at home I dream of long train rides with limitless time for reading (not with the two drunk young men who won't shut up in the quiet car, or young women with the shrieking cackle that carries). I dream of new tastes and smells and people, I don't think of myself cowering in my hotel room, trying to convince myself to get up and find food to eat.

When I am on the road, my home is a twinkling sanctuary of perfection. My lover is ideal, my friends are always around when I need them, I am paid on time for the freelance work that I do.

If I could twin myself, I would leave one at home to tend to the hearth, and the other would go out, Odysseus-like, to make her way across the sea. And they would play each role perfectly, archetypically, without messing it up with drippy nostalgia.

* * *

I am standing in the hotel hallway, because in my room there is a wasp. And it was fine when it was up in a corner, but it flew at my head and so I fled. Now I am not sure what to do. Maybe I can grab my pillow and just sleep out here, it doesn't look like it's at all interested in the open balcony door.

The man walks by and I imagine asks me what in the world I am doing. "Wasp," I tell him. No click of understanding, and so I use my fingers to create little antennae and I buzz around in a circle. "Wasp."

"*Ah!*" He walks straight into my room, pulls out a knife from his pocket, and stabs the wasp, killing it instantly.

Odysseus, I have found you.

"Come," he tells me, gesturing downward. "Eat."

The woman makes me a plate of food, greens and meat and

potatoes and tomatoes. She talks to me, going on in a language I don't understand, and I laugh when she laughs and nod when she pauses, smile encouragingly when she talks. I drench my plate in olive oil, my skin has never looked better, I am basically just drinking it out of the bottle now.

We seed pomegranates together, she moving twice as quickly as I do. My fingers stain ruby. When I go she makes up a bowl of seeds and almonds and golden raisins to take back upstairs as a snack. "Tomorrow?" she says, gesturing to the table. Tomorrow.

* * *

I am torn. I feel I could stay here forever. In the morning, I flip a coin. Heads, I go. Tails, I stay. Tails.

* * *

This past year, without a home to go back to, it's put nostalgia at bay, and I am beginning to think that maybe this is just how it is for me. Maybe never having had a city that felt like home means that I will never have a city that feels like home. If I flip it, that means all cities feel equally like home to me.

I really did think, setting out, that one city would speak to me, in that deep-down I-just-knew-I-was home way, like people who look across the room and say, "That is the man I am going to marry." I envy that certainty, and yet then there is always just that one thing forever and ever. I envy it in the way I envy my sister's children, my friends' marriages, my father's successful neighborhood business, in that if I ever actually had those things I would immediately look to lose them again.

I prefer to envy at a distance, where the edges are all so prettily blurred.

I was not gifted with a city on this journey, but I was gifted with something equally generous. The ability to move through the world.

* * *

In the morning, I flip a coin. Heads, I go. Tails, I stay. Tails.

* * *

I am back at the kitchen table, the son is here today. He is talking about the village, he thinks with some improvements they can attract the tourists back. Tourists now want organic things, they want natural, they want gourmet, they don't want cheap plastic. He can give them organic.

His mother is talking. I look at her and smile, but the son draws me back into conversation. He talks over his mother. His mother does not stop talking. The son looks at her, exasperated, but does not translate what she is saying. She looks down, sad.

He is talking about money again. He works here, at the hotel, he also works in the olive grove, and he does bookkeeping for a hotel in Athens. The man, he runs property, he also grows food for the market and makes wine and oil. The woman, she cleans another hotel and sews curtains and tablecloths. Everyone works many jobs, but there is no money.

The woman is talking again, still sad. The son finally translates: "She says she wishes she spoke English so she could understand the conversation." He laughs at her.

I touch her hand. We smile.

* * *

In the morning, I flip a coin. Heads, I go. Tails, I stay. Tails.

* * *

The village is nearly empty. There is one food market that remains open. Most of the restaurants have shuttered, to be opened again in the spring. A hotel down the road is still open, but when I walk past the lobby is always empty. There is only one other couple staying in my hotel. For an entire day I hear them fighting, fighting, fighting. The next day, I hear them having sex, sex, sex.

The lack of bathtub is the only thing keeping me from moving here permanently. I heat water in the electric kettle, pour it into a big bowl, and then use a cup and a washcloth and a bar of soap to clean myself. Or, the town empty, I walk into the sea naked and lie in the sun to dry.

I go into the city for dinner, eating pork with peppers and cheese and table wine. Most nights I am the only customer. The proprietor sends over free glasses of wine, extra courses, cheese, and bread. The combination of vulnerability and generosity sends me over the edge. This place is fragile. It will have to change again. It will have to start over, somehow. And these people, these people might hurt in the process. I feel it in me, I know the dark nights.

And yet the world is such a beautiful, wonderful place, I can't believe I ever thought of leaving it. Yes, I am drunk, but that does not negate the veracity of my statement.

* * *

In the morning, I flip a coin. Heads, I go. Tails, I stay. Tails.

* * *

That scene where Penelope finally recognizes her husband, it destroys me every time. That fight, of you are not my husband, you are not my husband, that refusal to recognize the thing you have been waiting so long for, it would be nice if a god did come down and say, This is that thing, stupid. The thing you have stared at the horizon waiting for for years now. It is standing right in front of you.

But it comes bearded and gnarled, it comes to us strangely.

And we shut our door, we say that is not it, go away, the real thing will be here any minute, shoo.

How many times have I turned away the thing that would save me? The gift bestowed, the gift unseen and rejected. I went looking for a family to take me in, I found a library full of ghosts instead. I went out looking for a home, I found the world instead.

*　*　*

In the morning, I flip a coin. Heads, I go. Tails, I stay. It's heads. It's time to go.

Suggested Reading

BERLIN / WILLIAM JAMES

Howard M. Feinstein, *Becoming William James*
Oliver Hilmes, *Cosima Wagner: The Lady of Bareuth*
Henry James, *A Small Boy and Others*
William James, *The Letters of William James*
　　Pragmatism and Other Writings
　　Varieties of Religious Experience
Alexandra Richie, *Faust's Metropolis: A History of Berlin*
Victor Sebestyen, *Revolution 1989: The Fall of the Soviet Empire*
Linda Simon, *Genuine Reality: A Life of William James*

TRIESTE / NORA BARNACLE

Sylvia Beach, *Shakespeare and Company*
Richard Francis Burton, *Personal Narrative of a Pilgrimage to*
　　Al-Madinah and Meccah
Ruth Butler, *Hidden in the Shadow of the Master: The Model-*
　　Wives of Cezanne, Monet, and Rodin
Michael Drury, *Advice to a Young Wife from an Old Mistress*
Richard Ellmann, *James Joyce*
Mary S Lovell, *A Rage to Live: A Biography of Richard and*
　　Isabel Burton
Claudio Magris, *Microcosms*
Brenda Maddox, *Nora: The Real Life of Molly Bloom*

Jan Morris, *Trieste and the Meaning of Nowhere*
Edna O'Brien, *Johnny I Hardly Knew You*

SARAJEVO / REBECCA WEST

BBC, *Death of Yugoslavia* (documentary film)
Miranda Carter, *George, Nicholas, and Wilhelm: Three Royal Cousins and the Road to World War I*
Zlatko Dizdarevic, *Sarajevo: A War Journal*
Victoria Glendinning, *Rebecca West: A Life*
Misha Glenny, *The Fall of Yugoslavia*
Susan Hertog, *Dangerous Ambition: Rebecca West and Dorothy Thompson*
Samantha Power, *A Problem from Hell: America and the Age of Genocide*
Laura Silber and Allan Little, *Yugoslavia: Death of a Nation*
Rebecca West, *Black Lamb and Grey Falcon*
  Henry James

SOUTH OF FRANCE / MARGARET ANDERSON

Margaret Anderson, *My Thirty Years War*
  The Strange Necessity
Holly A. Baggett, *Dear Tiny Heart*
Sylvia Beach, *Shakespeare and Company*
John Hoyte, *Trunk Road for Hannibal*
Jeffrey Segall, *Joyce in America*

GALWAY / MAUD GONNE

Nevill Drury, *Stealing Fire from Heaven: The Rise of Modern Western Magic*
Maud Gonne, *A Servant of the Queen: An Autobiography*
Mary K. Greer, *Women of the Golden Dawn: Rebels and Priestesses*

Mary Midgley, *Science and Poetry*
Thomas Nagel, *Mind and Cosmos*
Margaret Ward, *Maud Gonne: A Life*
W. B. Yeats, *The Autobiography of William Butler Yeats*

LAUSANNE / IGOR STRAVINSKY

Anne L Barstow, *Witchcraze*
Diccon Bewes, *Swiss Watching*
Ioan Culianu, *Eros and Magic in the Renaissance*
Bruce Gordon, *Calvin*
John McPhee, *La Place de la Concorde Suisse*
Igor Stravinsky, *An Autobiography*
    Poetics of Music in the Form of Six Lessons

ST. PETERSBURG / W. SOMERSET MAUGHAM

Selina Hastings, *The Secret Lives of Somerset Maugham*
Robert K Massie, *Peter the Great*
W. Somerset Maugham, *Ashenden*
    The Summing Up
    Cakes and Ale
Beverly Nichols, *A Case of Human Bondage*
John Reed, *The Ten Days That Shook the World*
Edmund Wilson, *To the Finland Station*

LONDON / JEAN RHYS

Lindsey German and John Rees, *A People's History of London*
Susan J. Matt, *Homesickness: An American History*
Iain McGilchrist, *The Master and His Emissary*
Carol Morley, dir., *Dreams of a Life*
Lillian Pizzichini, *The Blue Hour: A Life of Jean Rhys*
Jean Rhys, *Good Morning, Midnight*
    Voyage in the Dark

Kathy Acker, *In Memoriam to Identity*
  Pussycat Fever
Claude Cahun, *Disavowals: or Canceled Confessions*
Arthur Koestler, *Dialogue with Death*
Alan Riding, *And the Show Went On*
Louise Turner, ed., *Don't Kiss Me: The Art of Claude Cahun*
  and Marcel Moore
Peter Webb, *Sphinx: The Life and Art of Leonor Fini*